7-Day Dating
and Relationship Plan

for
Gay Men

Don,
Here's to a
stellar
dating year
for you!

Happy
dating!

Dennis
Courtney

Grant

The
7-Day
Dating and
Relationship Plan
for
Gay Men

Practical Advice
from the
Gay Matchmaker

Grant Wheaton
with Dennis Courtney

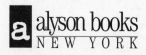

alyson books
NEW YORK

Manufactured in the United States of America

This trade paperback original is published by Alyson Books
245 West 17th Street, New York, NY 10011
Distribution in the United Kingdom by Turnaround Publisher Services Ltd.
Unit 3, Olympia Trading Estate, Coburg Road, Wood Green
London N22 6TZ England
First Edition: February 2008

08 09 10 11 12   a   10 9 8 7 6 5 4 3 2 1

ISBN: 1-59350-049-1
ISBN-13: 978-1-59350-049-8

Library of Congress Cataloging-in-Publication data are on file.
Cover design by Victor Mingovits
Interior design by Elliott Beard

CONTENTS

Introduction 1

PART I
THE 7-DAY PLAN

DAY 1   **Get Real and Be Honest**   9

DAY 2   **Live in the Now**   31

DAY 3   **Open Up and Extend**   45

DAY 4   **Balance**   55

DAY 5   **Be Patient, Responsible, and Respectful**   71

DAY 6   **Commit**   85

DAY 7   **Be Grateful and Enjoy!**   91

PART II
MORE PRACTICAL ADVICE
FROM THE GAY MATCHMAKER

CHAPTER 8   **Ask ManMate (including Top 10 Dating Tips)**   99

CHAPTER 9   **More Dating Tips**
                 (for First Dates, Blind Dates,
                 and All Dates, for That Matter)   113

CHAPTER 10   **Compatibility**   117

CHAPTER 11   **Where the Boys Are**   125

CHAPTER 12   **Fear versus Love**   129

CHAPTER 13   **My Story, in Brief**   137

                 Conclusion   141

                 Acknowledgments   143

                 About the Authors   145

The
7-Day Dating
and Relationship Plan
for
Gay Men

INTRODUCTION

Hey, guys—listen up! Here's an ongoing, doable Plan to help you work through all those dating woes—and find relationship success! The basic Plan is something you can incorporate into your life each week, with lots of flexibility.

Before we get down to it, let me introduce myself. I am the Gay Matchmaker. To be more specific, I was recently dubbed "the Dolly Levi for Gay New Yorkers" by the press (and, no, I do not look or talk like Carol Channing!).

As the founder/owner of ManMate, Inc., New York City's largest dating and relationship service for gay men, and as a workshop leader and coach, I have guided thousands of gay men through the often-treacherous trenches of dating. I've also seen hundreds of happy couples formed in the process.

Let me just say firsthand that, throughout over twenty years of extensive matchmaking I have encountered every situation imaginable. Because so many guys have become eager to confide in me and have felt free to speak from the heart, *I really have heard and seen it all!*

From the time I opened ManMate in June 1985 until the present, my approach to matching and introducing compatible men one-on-one has always been very personalized. Being casting director for Mr.

Right keeps me on my toes! I meet each client individually, which, believe it or not, is an oddity in today's dating scene, where the emphasis is on quick, iffy hookups from clubs, bars, and the Internet.

I like to get to the core of each client's unique situation: who he is, what truly makes him tick and, specifically, the sort of man who floats his boat regarding relationship potential. I then proceed to search for and introduce him to the most promising men possible, one at a time. Verbal and e-mail feedback is crucial, as together we zero in on his strongest candidates.

Many clients also have great success with our Dinners for 8 venue, where eight single, compatible men meet for the first time over drinks, dinner, and scintillating conversation. Again, that feedback keeps us narrowing it all down, one party to the next.

Of course, what makes me the most jazzed about what I do is the positive feedback I've gotten through the years. Here are some recent examples:

> "Marc is a wonderful guy. We have been dating for two months now. Thanks for your attentiveness in this process. I'm very grateful!"
> —Kurt S.

> "GREAT SELECTION—Chemistry was immediate!"
> —Bob H.

> "Incredible guy! This man has renewed my belief that an awesome guy is out there. I loved him. Handsome, smart, funny, well traveled, can talk about anything. All I can say is you hit the nail on the head. I could not be happier to have met him and hope this goes where I would like it to go. Thanks for the intro."
> —Alan C.

The following feedback was just about the most special I ever received. Sometimes the chemistry from my introductions leads to something really beautiful and lasting:

> "Hey there. My name is Jim C. I am currently living in Atlanta. I called and left a message on your voice mail because I would love to talk to you at some point about the man you introduced me to close to 20 years ago when your service was new.
>
> His name was Marty L. He was the first man's name you gave me, and we fell in love and stayed passionately in love until his death from AIDS on December 9, 2004. He was/is the absolute love of my life and I would have never met him had it not been for ManMate.
>
> I would love to tell you more about our wonderful life together.
>
> Thank you so much and I do hope I hear from you."
>
> **—Jim**

The challenges and rewards of my work that have continued to fascinate and energize me for over two decades are simply this: every guy I meet arrives with his own set of circumstances, preferences, strengths, weaknesses, fears—and, yes, sometimes major baggage. I work with him to help clear a path through a lot of today's insanity to develop a happy dating and love life. What could be better?

Let's get real (you'll hear me say that quite often—it's the ONLY path to successful dating). If we're being honest, many of us do have a fair amount of dating and relationship baggage. For those of us who grew up gay, there were few role models and not a lot of positive encouragement.

That was then . . . but times are definitely changing. Gay dating, gay marriage, gay rights, and gay relationships are hot topics all across the United States and the world, often being covered by the mainstream media. The success of TV shows such as *Will and Grace*, *Queer Eye for the Straight Guy*, and *Brothers and Sisters*, the emergence of LGBT networks, and the recent phenomenon of the film *Brokeback Mountain* exemplify the big push of gay consciousness out of the closet and into the mainstream.

We're just at the tip of the iceberg. This is not a mere phase, but the beginning of a new understanding—not only in the straight community but also within the gay community itself. I'm hopeful that we as gay men can now build on this understanding to find more fulfilling ways to date and love.

Combine this with the fact that all we have to do is pick up a popular magazine or turn on our TV to be amazed (or repulsed) at the current "makeover" fascination! We seem to have become obsessed with the notion that improving all the externals in our lives (physical looks, home makeovers, fashion and money status, material goods) will lead to happily-ever-after.

What about those men who have worked on those areas but are quite clueless about dating and spend a great deal of time depressed or suffering over the lack of love, sex, or romance in their lives? That's where I come in. In addition to being the Gay Matchmaker, I've become an expert at helping gay people of all types "make themselves over internally" for the dating and love relationships that are right for them.

In this age of instant gratification and "what's hot/what's not," we have followed all this advice found in the media to perfect all the externals in our lives. We even let America "vote" to determine our sexiness, eligibility, talent, and worth! Still, we've often found ourselves alone, when we've wanted it otherwise. With so much "help," why are there still so many lonely hearts looking to find and develop a meaningful relationship with Mr. Right? In our complex, diverse world, have we lost sight of the most basic truths and principles?

In response, I've devised *The 7-Day Dating and Relationship Plan for Gay Men*. Its proven principles can be applied successfully to all dating and relationship challenges. I use situations and people I have encountered as examples. (Of course, the names and places have been changed to protect the not-so-innocent! These examples may also be composites of several people in similar situations.)

This Plan is intended to be much more than a "What-to-Do-and-What-Not-to-Do-on-a-Date" lesson. It delves deeper to help you evolve in many areas of your life, making you a more desirable partner. I have found that so many dates fail even before they begin because the men simply aren't ready for the dating process. It is my sincerest hope that this Plan will be of enormous help to you.

In the *7-Day Dating and Relationship Plan for Gay Men*, there are seven principles to use for success. Amazing as it sounds, I can guarantee you that all your dating issues are covered by applying one or more of these principles.

It's simple—you focus on only one principle per day for each day of the week (or one per week if focusing on one per day is too intense). For example, if you start on Sunday as Day 1, your focus could be on principle 1—Get Real and Be Honest. The next day, Monday, you move on to principle 2—Live in the Now, and so on through the week. When Sunday comes around again, you're back to focusing on Get Real and Be Honest.

If you prefer, you can shuffle the order of the principles week to week, depending on the energy of your life in that particular week. You can even repeat a principle on more than one day and skip the one it replaced for that particular week, if that is more effective.

If you find that there are one or more particular areas in which you have a block, you might want to concentrate more on these areas. I would avoid skipping any one principle too often, however, as it can reduce the effectiveness of this Plan.

Can more than one principle be applied on any given day? Of course! You'll learn to tap into your instincts as to when to emphasize more than one on certain days. They are there to serve you. As long as you continue to refer to and tap into all seven principles on an ongoing basis, you'll find dating and relationship success. Plus, with the principles as your guide, you can start fresh every week!

As the weeks go by, you'll get to know these dating principles quite intimately. You will also become more aware of how to utilize each one as you learn to more fully tap into your instincts. You can use the exercises provided at the end of each chapter on an ongoing basis. I strongly recommend giving yourself a few minutes at the beginning of each day to review the exercises you've chosen for that day.

The issue at the core of each specific dating challenge you face may not seem clear right away. Yet I've found that, using one or more of these principles, you can figure it out and make a positive choice for yourself in any given moment. You can move through each fear or frustration, however significant or seemingly trivial, to a place where you can eventually create a relationship that brings you satisfaction, joy, and fulfillment. Let's get real: After all is said and done . . . and done . . . and done . . . that's what we all eventually want.

Along the way, trust your own unique qualities, sense of fun, and dating gaydar as you navigate through a maze of hunks, geeks, jocks, freaks, princes, queens, tops, bottoms, versatiles, butches, bitches, bisexuals, dorks, daddies, twinks, trannies, bears, cubs, masters, slaves, drag queens, preppies, thugs, gypsies, tramps, and thieves or any of the wonderful combinations out there to find your own Mr. Right!

PART I

The
7-Day Plan

DAY 1

Get Real *and* Be Honest

Do you really want a relationship? If so, are you clear about who you are, what you are willing to give, and what you expect from a partner?

Have you thought about what type of relationship may be right for you?

Are you simply following the mating trends we've been taught by our straight community and pop culture, or have you begun to identify your own unique path?

Take some time to consider the questions above. Are you able to answer them readily and with certainty? If you were to be asked some very basic questions about your career (method of work, goals, priorities, etc.), you'd probably be able to answer them confidently and in detail. It's really the only way to be successful at your job. So why is it that similar questions about relationships and dating puzzle so many?

Some men may not want to be in a love relationship. There is certainly nothing wrong with that choice. Before we go any further, take the time now to determine whether or not you want a relationship. If you are really just looking for the hottest sex around or want to play the field, then by all means be honest and go for it—get your freak on and have a great time! (Safely, of course.) But, don't pretend you're willing to focus on a potential, full-fledged relationship beyond the physical. It's the dishonest, game-playing, cowardly, misleading men out there who cause a lot of emotional pain and give the rest of us a bad name. (There—I've said it!)

Since you're reading this Plan, I'm assuming you're interested in finding the type of relationship that's right for you. To be successful in finding that relationship, isn't it important to first get real about yourself and what you're looking for?

Gay men have varying definitions of a relationship, which makes finding the ideal date or partner more challenging. Because our views about dating and relationships can be so different, it's probably safe to say there is no model.

Getting real about your own desires is the first and most essential step. What do I mean by that? Getting real means discovering or rediscovering your authentic self and having the integrity to present that true self to those with whom you interact.

In this world obsessed with physical beauty, youth, image, façade, popularity, celebrity, and political correctness, it may often seem that just being your unique self is not enough or even unacceptable. Nothing could be further from the truth. Success in relationships and other areas of our lives comes only when we have the courage to embrace our uniqueness.

If you get only one point from this book, let it be the following:

You must get real and honest about yourself—the best and the worst—and accept yourself as the complete package that you are. Complete does not mean perfect. We are all works in progress. Complete is the acknowledgment of the authentic you—all aspects. If you are looking for someone else to complete you, you will not find yourself in a healthy, fulfilling relationship.

I'm sure you've heard that before and already understand it intellectually, but it is imperative that you really get it on a deeper, more
visceral level. It takes a real commitment to examine our lives and
the patterns we've developed in dating and relationships and then to
make a conscious effort to change and improve.

My past twenty-plus years of work have shown me that if you are
not being real about yourself, you are not ready for a relationship. It is
as simple as that. The rest of this book will be of little use unless you
are willing to grasp this concept. It is what you bring of your authentic
self to a date or relationship that makes it exciting.

Don't cheat yourself or others by assuming you are only as good
as your physical looks. If you are not clear about and assured of your
total self and your desires, you will not bring much to the table in a
dating or relationship scenario besides being eye candy. You will only
be presenting a façade, which may get you laid and be interesting for
a while, but will have little lasting power.

My belief in the importance of being authentic was strongly affirmed recently by my friend, Griffin, who came to my office over fifteen years ago and became a client. I introduced him to several men
over a period of time and nothing seemed to click.

Recently, over lunch, Griffin told me that when he first came to
me he thought he was ready for a relationship, but as I encouraged
him to get real about what he wanted, he realized that he didn't really
desire a full-fledged relationship. As he put it, "I just didn't want to
be alone during the holidays." Eventually, when he was ready, I introduced him to his current partner, Stewart, and they've been together
for over ten years.

Larry Loser

> "When I go out with a guy, I just tell him I'm very well off and have this fabulous career. That way I'll hook him, and he won't think I'm a total loser. No one would ever want to be with the real me."
>
> —Larry Loser

Recently, I've been hearing the word "loser" used more and more by people to describe others they've dated or how they're currently feeling about themselves. "What a loser!" "All I ever attract are losers!" "Oh boy, another loser of the week!" Loser. Loser. Loser. It has become a trendy description for any displeasing character trait. We quickly use the word to describe the other person when a date or even a relationship goes bad. But, what specifically do we mean?

My definition of a "loser" is one who lacks the confidence to be real. As a result, he loses his true self. He has a fear that being real will not be enough and that he will ultimately be rejected.

I'll be the first to acknowledge that many gay men reject potential dates or relationships based solely on superficialities. That's their problem—it doesn't have to be yours. When you "fall in love at first sight" with that gorgeous guy you meet, look further than the beautiful eyes, perfect jawline, broad shoulders, big pecs, slim waist, six-pack abs, round butt, and perfect penis to a more important consideration—ask yourself if he seems ready for a deeper, meaningful relationship that goes past the external. You can only move into a successful dating relationship with him if the answer is "yes." Otherwise, you might enjoy the view and have a fun roll in the sack, but leave it at that.

Whether we acknowledge it or not, we all have an internal BS barometer that reacts when we encounter someone who is not being real. We know when someone is not expressing his own values, opinions, needs, style, image, or voice. Our instincts tell us to avoid that guy. Listen to those instincts or suffer the consequences later.

We've all encountered people we thought were losers, or people who might have thought the same of us (ouch!). Let's look at some real examples of people I've worked with and the advice I've given them.

Max MixedMessages

> "All I want is a man to share my life. You know, someone who has some of the same values and interests. But not like the last guy I dated! We're not at all in the same social circles. The kid never had any money, so, yeah, I always paid his way. He was crazy about me. But I had to end it with him. Well, actually he broke up with me, but, whatever..."
>
> —Max MixedMessages

Sometimes I feel like the Simon Cowell of dating! In my line of work, I do have a unique vantage point. When people come in to work with me, they usually want to put their best foot forward, and even in spite of themselves I'm able to see the reality of who they are. I get a true picture of how they come across to other people. When you're dating and meeting others for the first time, first impressions are very important. Yet it amazes me sometimes how my clients will have such an inaccurate picture of who they really are.

Max came into my office recently to become a client. At first he seemed very gregarious and incredibly friendly—a social kind of guy with a huge network of "friends."

Within a minute or two I realized Max was already doing his "shtick," in full performance mode. I have a small, intimate office, and this man could have blown the walls out with the volume of his voice. He was working the balcony! He's definitely a master of networking, a very successful entrepreneur, and also very obviously on the flamboyant side. I would humorously describe him as a cross between Richard Simmons and Rosie O'Donnell!

Max told me he was thirty-nine years old. I would have guessed he was verging on fifty. Early in the conversation, he told me a straight friend swore to him that if there was a room full of one hundred men, Max would be the last one people would imagine was gay. My jaw almost dropped, but then I remembered that I needed to be respectful of my client.

Max then went on to tell me about a series of boyfriends he had had that were all at least half his age. He also made it clear that he had been the one to break off with each of them. In the same breath, he let it be known that even though he had footed the bill for all these previous involvements (Sugar Daddy, anyone?), he was very interested in a full-fledged relationship now.

By this time I was so overwhelmed with all his bluster and mixed messages that I had to pause for a moment to sort it all out. What I was hearing from him was, "On the one hand, I'd like a real relationship with an equal partner, but on the other hand, I'm still intrigued by younger men, and as soon as I decide they've worn out their usefulness, I'll go pay for a newer model."

I haven't yet had a serious conversation with Max about getting real. But by the time you read this, I will have. Between you and me, what I'd really like to say is, "Just be honest—if what you really want is a revolving door of boy toys, then admit it and just go for that. But, if you're really serious about something more substantial with a man you can truly relate to as a peer, then you clearly need to shift gears."

This is a tough one. I often hear a person saying that they want a relationship, but find it hard to resist a younger plaything who is really unsuited to be an equal partner. I did sense that a part of Max was being very sincere. . . . I'm going to appeal to that side.

Wish me luck!

Adam ApprovalJunkie

> "This outfit costs more than my rent. So what?
> It looks great on me, right?" . . . "All this talk
> about issues doesn't matter. I just want him to
> like me." . . . "Do you think other guys are at-
> tracted to me?"
>
> **—Adam ApprovalJunkie**

In every waking moment, Adam, a man I've coached, seems concerned about what people think of him. He's in endless pursuit of approval. (I can tell you from my experience with him that his constant
need for approval is exhausting!) Every man whom Adam meets becomes his reality base for judging himself—how he should be or act.
Out of fear of not being affirmed by each man, Adam tries to become
the fantasy figure he thinks the man might want and does not present his true self.

Adam is continually talking himself up and exaggerating his accomplishments. He never delves into what he himself really wants or
really feels. Instead, he decides he must somehow inflate his image to
impress others. (Right about now, you may be hearing your own inner
voice asking if you've known people like Adam. Perhaps you've be-
haved this way? Listen to this voice—it knows the answer.)

My advice to Adam began with a series of questions. I asked him
to share his opinions about everything from his favorite color to his
political and spiritual convictions. What made him feel elated? What
pissed him off? He found it quite difficult to give a definitive answer
to each question.

Adam's lack of clarity let me know that he had yet to determine
what it was in life that defined his sensibilities and made him tick. He
had been wary of expressing these opinions because, in his reasoning,
it was easier to gain approval without having a strong sense of himself.
Once he started to regain his lost identity by defining his opinions and
boundaries, he became aware (ta-da!) that he had been doing nothing
to gain his own approval.

Paul Pushover

> "I get so nervous when there's tension in the air. Why can't everyone just be as agreeable as I am?"
> —Paul Pushover

Adam and Max are admittedly extreme examples of people I've known who have had to work hard at getting real. There are certainly many less extreme examples. Some people choose to play the part of "the pushover" (or "doormat" or "wimp").

The pushover constantly acquiesces to someone else. He is not strong in his own resolve. He feels that his job is to always agree (he's into "S&N"—smile and nod) and to keep everything light and easy, even if his true self might disagree. It is the pushover's desire to please at any cost.

This type of behavior has also been called the "disease to please." Ironically, it has been my observation that these men tend to be less valued and respected by others, who perceive them as weak. Essentially, pushovers lose by compromising their own true feelings to avoid discord.

I do believe that compromise is important in relationships. But if you are always trying to make the other person comfortable, you may be denying or even avoiding your own point of view. We're usually drawn to those with a strong sense of conviction, whatever their personality. Getting real about how you perceive yourself and how you really stand on issues will help you fulfill the true potential of any situation.

David Dishonest

> "Alright, alright, so I lied about my stats in my online profile. You should see the stud who responded—he wants to meet this weekend. . . . Oh my God! What do I do now? I'm screwed!"
> **—David Dishonest**

Sound familiar? Let's talk about lying, shall we? It would be an understatement to say that dishonesty plays a huge role in destroying dating opportunities and relationships. I often find this subject difficult, but crucial to broach with clients as we approach getting real.

It's amazing how many ways we all have to justify our untruths. In this age where everything seems to be spun and manipulated, where so-called role models and leaders lie for advancement and other self-interests, it might seem easier to just go with the flow of deception. But, the consequences of dishonesty are enormous. I could write an entire book based solely on the disasters I've witnessed in dishonest relationships, and I'm sure each of you reading this could tell your own horror stories. Being dishonest, whether by withholding the truth or telling an outright lie, is so incredibly destructive.

We all know guys who are simply liars. I don't care how cute, hot, or adorable they might seem, because eventually their lives become a mess of deceptions. Their reputations precede them, and ultimately they become completely undesirable. Clearly, they're not on the path to honest and successful relationships.

The simple truth? There cannot be a completely authentic connection with a liar. In every situation, reality eventually sets in and the truth reveals itself. Any façade, lie, or deceit eventually causes pain, anger, and frustration, not to mention time wasted, which cannot be relived.

These days there seems to be an unspoken tolerance for, and even acceptance of, lying. Just because it has become commonplace and often expected, doesn't mean that it's OK to be a liar. You think I'm overreacting or being unrealistic or even judgmental? OK, then keep on lying, Chicken Little, and see how long it takes the sky to fall on your head!

All bitchiness aside, I truly believe that becoming more honest takes "getting real" to a deeper level. When you date a man with the potential for a relationship, resolve to be more direct, clear, and honest in your communication and look for the same from him.

Day 1 Weekly "Get Real and Be Honest" Exercises

Let's presume you have decided to get real and to more fully reveal your true self. *Bravo!* Now, the first question to ask yourself is: "What is it about the real me that is unique?"

Let's start with the physical, since our physical self is the first thing others see. Rule number one: *Do not compare yourself with others!* I wish this were a law! It's the absolute worst thing you can do; yet we all struggle with this.

Begin by taking stock of yourself as an individual unlike all others. What are your best physical traits? Don't cop out by saying that there are none. No pity parties allowed! People have varied tastes, and there are people out there who find you attractive. (Now's the time to turn off that doubting voice in your head!)

Below you'll find a place to list five of your most favorable physical characteristics. You might ask, "Why should I make a list?" My answer: The list is a commitment to start an action. It's the beginning of a plan. It's good to hope and wish and dream, but hopes and wishes and dreams aren't actions.

So, no excuses—you don't even have to look for a blank sheet of paper—just grab a pencil. If you have more than five, then more power to you! Go ahead and continue the list on a separate sheet of paper. If you find less than five, write those down and know you'll add more in the future as you find power in complimenting yourself.

As you compile this list, you'll discover more and more attractive and even sexy features. Perhaps you have great hair, beautiful eyes or skin, a stunning nose, or an amazing, sensual mouth. Do people compliment your smile? You may have a strong or graceful gait when you walk. You could have impressive biceps or a butt that can stop traffic. View yourself from top to bottom! Really take the time to compliment yourself.

If this exercise makes you feel awkward or uncomfortable, then you definitely need to do it! Have fun and don't be afraid to be detailed and candid. No one has to read this list but you, so what the hell! Go for it.

My Five Most Favorable Physical Characteristics

1. _____

2. _____

3. _____

4. _____

5. _____

Now, allow yourself to see these features as gifts you have been given and can share with others. Be proud of them and make the most of them. Continue to improve your body, externally and internally. Believe me, there are people out there who not only find you desirable but also may be envious of your physical self.

This process may seem hard at first. We are often conditioned as children to be self-effacing: "Don't brag," "Don't come off as too confident," and even "Get over yourself!" What a bunch of bull! Be assured of your best physical traits. Be confident. Confidence, not cockiness, is very attractive and very sexy.

But what about the physical characteristics that make you unhappy or maybe even miserable? This is a very touchy subject. Many men continue to use negative traits to justify fear or as excuses for unhappiness and failure. This may not be the most fun list to compile, but getting real allows you to move away from fear and loser behavior.

If you are dealing with self-esteem issues, as many of us are, this list could get quite long very quickly. Before you revert to tearing yourself apart, remember, no one, to my knowledge, is perfectly satisfied with his looks or body. (If you find such a man, please let me—and the *Guinness Book of World Records*—know.) If they were, the number of gym memberships, plastic surgeries, and sales of cosmetics would not be so enormous.

When taking stock of our less desirable traits, it is imperative to determine what can or cannot be changed. Keeping this in mind, go ahead and fill in the list of five. If you insist there are more than five, then continue the list on a separate sheet of paper. (I'm really hoping that won't be necessary.)

My Five Most Challenging Physical Characteristics
(Notice I didn't say "negative" or "unfavorable." Neither should you.)

1. _____

2. _____

3. _____

4. _____

5. _____

Now that you've completed the list, take a good look at it. Decide which things you can improve in a healthy, realistic manner. Now, really listen to your inner voice and be honest. Do you want to make these changes to please someone else? If so—*stop! Do not pass go! Do not collect $200!* Definitely rethink the situation. If your inner voice is screaming at you to make changes to feel better about yourself, to become healthier, or to boost your self-esteem, then go for it.

For example, let's say you are dissatisfied with your hair, or lack of it. After deciding you'd like to change this situation, you could possibly consult a stylist. If you are a balding man, there are many stylists who are experts in hairpieces or hair replacement. (Please, if you chose this route, go to an expert! A bad piece is way too scary.) You may also consider shaving your head. It's a very hot look right now!

With a little creative thinking, there are so many ways to improve. Take these challenges one at a time. That way it won't seem so overwhelming.

Five Corresponding Ways to Improve Each of My Challenging Physical Characteristics

1. _____

2. _____

3. _____

4. _____

5. _____

Now, congratulate yourself for making the first important step in improving your physical self!

Weight is often a major issue, but it is also something you can control. Again, be realistic. You may not be meant have a 30-inch waist. But you can make the choice to be at the best weight for you. If you have doubts, consult an expert and proceed in a healthy manner.

You might also want to update or completely revamp your wardrobe. Again, this should be a decision made to please only you. If having new clothes will make you feel more confident and you can afford them without breaking the bank, then by all means, head on out to the store. Take a good, trusted friend with you for moral support and make it an adventure. Your buddy might also have some great ideas.

Dealing with other physical attributes may be more difficult. Obviously, if you are an adult, you can't add or subtract inches from your height the same way you lose or gain weight. So, make the best of your height situation. If you are a short man, having a Napoleon complex will not help you win friends or influence people. Just look how he ended up!

Walking tall with confidence and dressing for a longer look will bring about more pleasing results. Just think of the many shorter men who have gone on to greatness in spite of their stature. This under 5'9" crew currently consists of Martin Short (no pun intended), Dustin Hoffman, Michael J. Fox, and Matthew Broderick, to name just a few.

I use these men as examples not only because they are familiar to us and have achieved professional success, but also because they are involved in successful personal relationships. (Some might argue that it is easy to find love and romance when you are rich and famous. If that argument really held water, the divorce rate of the rich and famous wouldn't be so staggeringly high!) These men have made the best of themselves, despite their height. We could find countless examples of not-so-famous men as well.

In contrast, taller men who walk around slump-shouldered don't appear shorter. They simply look meek and defeated. What I'm saying is, wear your size with pride—short or tall. You can't change it physiologically, so get over it and make it work for you.

Many people are displeased with their facial features. Again, be realistic. We were not all born to be magazine models. However, if your face is really creating misery for you and everyday maintenance or cosmetics haven't helped you feel better, consult a professional.

Plastic surgery is certainly an option. But consider it only if it will make you feel better about your appearance and increase your confidence as a result. If you are thinking of plastic surgery only to please some guy or as a result of a comparison to another man—*don't!* Plastic surgery has been a blessing for many who approach it for the right reasons and a disappointment for those who have unrealistic expectations of becoming instantly attractive.

Let's move on past the physical (please!). Getting real about your appearance is only one aspect. After all, we're the most highly evolved creatures (even gym bunnies!) because we exist on many levels beyond the physical. We communicate on a sophisticated level (OK—maybe not gym bunnies!), expressing a full array of feelings and traits. We all have desirable and undesirable characteristics. To feel complete, we need to acknowledge all facets of our personalities.

Take stock of all your positive traits. Are you a great listener? Maybe you have an unparalleled gift for conversation. Are you a computer whiz or a talented musician? Again, fill in the list below with your best traits. Don't hold back. Be as complete in your description as possible. Have that extra sheet of paper ready in case you need to list more.

My Five Most Favorable Non-Physical Characteristics

1. _____

2. _____

3. _____

4. _____

5. _____

Now, consider ways to make the best use of these characteristics. You may be surprised to find that you are indeed very interesting, when you allow these traits to surface and become an everyday part of your expression.

Now it's time to get real about your less positive traits. Don't deny or hide from these traits. Perhaps you have a temper or tend to be defensive. Maybe you are perceived as being too judgmental or intolerant. Are you too pushy? (For some reason, I can identify with that one . . .) We all have our own challenges. Take a deep breath, and honestly confront your not-so-attractive aspects.

My Five Most Challenging Non-Physical Characteristics

1. _____

2. _____

3. _____

4. _____

5. _____

Working through these challenges on a continual basis in a healthy manner can bring about a tremendous sense of victory and self-esteem and make you a much more attractive person. For example, you might have the annoying habit of interrupting people before they've finished speaking. Although you might say it comes from a genuine sense of excitement and energy, it is still off-putting to others.

You can make a conscious choice today to really listen to people and not jump in until they have finished. Try breathing and relaxing as you listen. It's so easy in today's rushed world to get ahead of the moment. (We'll talk about this further in Day 2 of the Plan).

Give this same thought to all the challenges you listed and now make a conscious effort to improve them. If you have a debilitating problem, making the courageous choice to seek professional help can seem like a victory in itself.

Five Choices I'm Making Now to Change and Improve My Challenging Non-Physical Characteristics

1. _____

2. _____

3. _____

4. _____

5. _____

Deal Breakers?

Now that we've spent some time focusing on you, let's begin thinking about your connection with potential dates or partners. Consider what type of relationship you're ultimately looking for. Gay men tend to be very clear about their tastes and needs in most other areas of their life. So I continually find it surprising that men will date, have sex, and fall in love with men who have completely incompatible relationship goals. Differences in other areas can be exciting and fulfilling, but it is crucial that you and your partner share some basic relationship goals. Otherwise—potential disaster!

You'll be responding to the following statements by checking one of the following:

❑ Agree
❑ Agree somewhat
❑ Neutral
❑ Disagree somewhat
❑ Disagree

Be honest with your answers. There's nothing to gain by deceiving yourself. You might not have a definite answer, and that's OK.

The point is to begin to clarify your needs honestly. The answers may reveal themselves later in your process.

1. **I have definite views about what a relationship should be.**
   - ❑ Agree
   - ❑ Agree somewhat
   - ❑ Neutral
   - ❑ Disagree somewhat
   - ❑ Disagree

2. **Monogamy is a crucial aspect of relationship success.**
   - ❑ Agree
   - ❑ Agree somewhat
   - ❑ Neutral
   - ❑ Disagree somewhat
   - ❑ Disagree

3. **I am a one-man-at-a-time man.**
   - ❑ Agree
   - ❑ Agree somewhat
   - ❑ Neutral
   - ❑ Disagree somewhat
   - ❑ Disagree

4. **I need to spend a great deal of time with my partner(s).**
   - ❑ Agree
   - ❑ Agree somewhat
   - ❑ Neutral
   - ❑ Disagree somewhat
   - ❑ Disagree

5. **I would enjoy raising a child with my partner.**
   - ❏ Agree
   - ❏ Agree somewhat
   - ❏ Neutral
   - ❏ Disagree somewhat
   - ❏ Disagree

6. **It is important for my partner to be quite social.**
   - ❏ Agree
   - ❏ Agree somewhat
   - ❏ Neutral
   - ❏ Disagree somewhat
   - ❏ Disagree

7. **Sex is very important.**
   - ❏ Agree
   - ❏ Agree somewhat
   - ❏ Neutral
   - ❏ Disagree somewhat
   - ❏ Disagree

8. **With regard to sex, quantity is most important.**
   - ❏ Agree
   - ❏ Agree somewhat
   - ❏ Neutral
   - ❏ Disagree somewhat
   - ❏ Disagree

9. **With regard to sex, quality is most important.**
   - ❏ Agree
   - ❏ Agree somewhat
   - ❏ Neutral
   - ❏ Disagree somewhat
   - ❏ Disagree

10. **I am absolute about sexual preferences or roles.**
    - ❑ Agree
    - ❑ Agree somewhat
    - ❑ Neutral
    - ❑ Disagree somewhat
    - ❑ Disagree

11. **I am open to a mixed-status relationship, regarding HIV (one partner being HIV+ and the other partner being HIV-).**
    - ❑ Agree
    - ❑ Agree somewhat
    - ❑ Neutral
    - ❑ Disagree somewhat
    - ❑ Disagree

12. **I consider myself bisexual. That preference will have to fit into my relationship(s).**
    - ❑ Agree
    - ❑ Agree somewhat
    - ❑ Neutral
    - ❑ Disagree somewhat
    - ❑ Disagree

13. **I could possibly have a long-distance relationship.**
    - ❑ Agree
    - ❑ Agree somewhat
    - ❑ Neutral
    - ❑ Disagree somewhat
    - ❑ Disagree

14. **My partner and I should be in a similar income bracket.**
    - ❑ Agree
    - ❑ Agree somewhat
    - ❑ Neutral
    - ❑ Disagree somewhat
    - ❑ Disagree

15. **My partner and I should have similar spiritual/religious convictions.**
    - ❑ Agree
    - ❑ Agree somewhat
    - ❑ Neutral
    - ❑ Disagree somewhat
    - ❑ Disagree

16. **It is important for my partner to be out regarding his sexuality.**
    - ❑ Agree
    - ❑ Agree somewhat
    - ❑ Neutral
    - ❑ Disagree somewhat
    - ❑ Disagree

Now, review your responses to get an idea of the direction of your dating and relationship needs. The result will be an important reference point for the rest of the Plan.

Good work! Pat yourself on the back for making these crucial first steps.

Once a week, you can refer back to this "Get Real and Be Honest" section to reevaluate your progress, perhaps to make different lists according to your changing needs and observations and to give yourself a fresh perspective. But for now, let's move on to the rest of *The 7-Day Dating and Relationship Plan.*

> **"When someone sees the real you and wants to share his life with you . . . that's powerful."**
> **—Author unknown**

DAY 2

Live *in the* Now

> "He was the love of my life. I'm not gonna find
> someone that great again."
> —Yanni Yesterday

Oh, the drama! Even before a guy has the chance to make this clichéd statement (and believe me, I hear it a lot!), I can tell when he's stuck in the past. I recognize the look in his eyes—glazed over, sad, still nursing old feelings. In my profession, it's a look I see often.

Unfortunately, it's also the look that his potential dates see. He just can't seem to move forward. He'll go on a first date and proceed to talk about his last boyfriend and then ask me why the guy didn't call him again.

Here's a recent response, almost verbatim, from one of my clients, after meeting a "Yanni Yesterday" type:

> "I couldn't believe it! Here we are, our first date
> at a romantic little bistro. Tony's a very hot, at-
> tractive guy, and I could tell he was into me. So
> why does he spend the whole dinner telling me

about his ex from two years ago? Guess I'm not
so into him after all."
—Frank Frustrated

Nix the Ex-Talk

Talk about self-sabotage! What could be more misguided on a first,
potentially romantic date, than a chat about Mr. Wonderful from the
Past? Later on in this Plan, I'll be sharing a few "dos and don'ts" regarding first dates. However, here's a no-brainer preview: *Don't talk
about an ex-boyfriend on a first date!*

Most of us with any relationship history have faced this temptation, especially after our first, real relationship, whether it lasted six
weeks, six months, six years, or longer. Maybe we created something
really beautiful and meaningful with an ex. Or maybe he turned into
the asshole of the universe, and we want the entire universe to know
it! Good news or bad news, discussion of our ex should be saved for
our close, non-romantic friends—or a therapist.

(Note: I'm not talking about guys who are coming out of a recently
ended relationship. There is, of course, an entire emotional process
to go through, including a grieving period in which we do reflect on
and learn from the past. Anyone going through this should probably
not be dating. I'm referring to men who are well beyond the process
after a breakup and continue to be mired in and often obsessed with
the past.)

Listen, Listen, Listen

So how do you get past the temptation and change this old behavior?
The first and most important step is—*listen*. Are you hearing me?
That's right—simply listen. Listen to what he is actually saying in that

very moment—and how he is saying it. Not what you wish or think he is saying.

Also, without exception, listen to your own inner voice (or common sense—or instinct—whatever you call it) to make the most of this encounter. You're there with him now. Doesn't it make sense to make the most of the meeting, regardless of what happens later?

While we're on the subject, don't mentally compare him to an ex (easier said than done, but don't). This type of comparison is not only masochistic but will freeze you in past pain. No guy you meet will ever be good enough for you (or your mother), you'll move back home, sequester yourself in your childhood bedroom, light a candle for him every night, and then . . . oh my God! . . . OK, that might be a bit extreme, but you get my point?

Here's a related story—a bit less dramatic, but true.

Timothy

Timothy leveled with me from the moment he came into my office. He had completely focused on his medical career for the past decade, and he now had a very successful practice to show for it. At forty-five, he also hadn't had a date in over ten years.

Interestingly enough, while in his twenties, Timothy had had three different relationships, each lasting about two years. He passionately recounted how beautiful and wonderful his past loves were. He had a collection of photos he was eager to show me of him with each of his trio of exes. Each was strikingly handsome, in an Abercrombie and Fitch type of way.

Based on his current appearance, I wouldn't have recognized Timothy as the same vibrant man that I saw in the photos. The past decade-plus of his dedicated career work had taken its toll on him. I could see he had put on about fifty pounds, had lost a good deal of his hair, and, somewhere along the way, had mislaid some very basic grooming tips. Before I had a chance to ask him about the sort of man he was looking to meet, Timothy informed me that what he was now seeking was—can you guess?—an Abercrombie and Fitch type in his twenties!

I was tempted to remind him that he did not have a portrait of Dorian Gray aging in the attic while he remained unchanged throughout the years, but I restrained myself. Although perhaps not to this extreme, I've heard some variation on this scenario from my clients and students more times than I can count over the past two decades.

The guy in each scenario has had, as many of us have had, an incredibly passionate first love, or perhaps more than one passionate love, often in his twenties. It was, or seemed so at the time, life transforming! Because of the intense, even intoxicating feelings he experienced at that time, each man wants to recapture that increasingly elusive, passionate rush by maintaining essentially the same criteria, including age, for any prospective future partners. In essence, his dream partner hasn't aged or changed, but the man clearly has.

Other Age Issues

Another variation on the age issue I've frequently come across involves the recently married gay man, often a father. He has remained closeted and married during his twenties or thirties, sometimes even into his forties or fifties. Finally he comes to grips with being gay, comes out of the closet, and proceeds to explore his repressed sexuality, often with wild abandon. Because his exploration with men has been virtually nonexistent for many years, he frequently gravitates toward much younger partners. After all, he never had the opportunity to experience his sexuality when he was their age. He may even feel inadequate because of his lack of experience. But even though these young guys may share his basic level of sexual enthusiasm and inexperience, they usually don't have much else in common.

Here's yet another prevalent age scenario. My associate, Greg Miller, the host and general manager of ManMate Dinners for 8, and I confer regularly on seating our dinner parties as compatibly as possible. Recently, we've both been noticing how frequently dinner party members, usually in their forties and fifties, stipulate that they would only like to meet men who are their own age or younger. Even more restrictive are the clients who only want to meet men at least eight to ten years younger—or even more.

I can't help but wonder, when they are eight to ten years older themselves, whether the age range of potential candidates for these men will remain frozen in time. Many of them insist that they never meet men their own age who are as youthful looking, thinking, or acting as they are. I personally think that it has more to do with genuinely accepting and liking themselves for who they are and where they are in their lives. Plus, of course, living in the now.

That reminds me of a certain Dinners for 8 client . . .

Gordon

We seated Gordon, age sixty-five, for his first dinner party with seven other men who were all, as he requested, five to ten years younger. When we received his feedback, we found that he was dissatisfied because he felt the men at the party had been too old for him.

(As a side note, let me say that when Gordon had originally submitted a photo of himself, I thought my eyesight was out of whack. Then I realized the photograph was in such soft focus that it was hard to distinguish Gordon's actual facial features. Not since Lucille Ball in the movie musical *Mame* has there been so much gauze put over a camera lens!)

Gordon now wanted to adjust his original age stipulations. He declared that he was not interested in meeting anyone over the age of forty-five! Since the dinner party seating is based on eight men having a degree of compatibility and chemistry, I had to ask myself, "Where and when will Gordon fit in with seven other men all young enough to be his sons?"

How did we handle this, you might ask? Well, carefully. . . . We explained the challenge to Gordon and emphasized that he would have to be very patient until the right group came along. *Ver-r-r-ry* patient. It could happen. . . . One never knows . . .

I do not feel that a large age difference is necessarily a negative aspect in a gay relationship. In fact, I have a gay cousin, Steven, who has been with his partner, Leonard, who is exactly twenty years older, for over twenty-five years. I admire their incredible, thriving relationship. But when I see my clients only pursuing the energy and images of much younger men in an attempt to recapture their youth, having little else in common, I know the results will inevitably prove to be quite lonely for them.

The Good News

OK. Enough digressing! Back to the two of you—you and the new guy—and bringing out the best of your date. In addition to listening and really hearing him, consider the promising aspects of the connection between the two of you.

First, and most obvious, what is pleasing to you about him? Do you like the way he's dressed or a particular article of clothing or accessory he's wearing? Does he have a winning smile or a great haircut? Whatever it is, compliment him. What could get your meeting off to a better start? Who doesn't like to be genuinely complimented?

Next, move on to other subjects. Let's tune into maximizing the quality of the meeting. What interests do you share? What do you both have in common that you really care about? Begin to notice how your personalities mesh. How can you instinctively bring out his strongest points? Listen moment to moment—the clues are there as you continue to focus on him and make the most of this new connection.

At my dating service, ManMate, we send each of our clients a brief Introduction Feedback Form. It gives each guy a chance to assess each one-on-one introduction he meets through us. In addition to telling us more specifically what works and doesn't work for him, it inevitably clues us in on the behavior of his date.

Essentially, the feedback ratings about each date's attentiveness and sensitivity tell me how much the date was "living in the now" with his introduction. Not surprisingly, the guys I've worked with who get the most positive, ongoing feedback from their matches have eventually achieved the best relationship success. Here's a perfect example:

Alex and Josh

About four years ago, I introduced my client Alex to a series of promising candidates. Alex was thirty-four and an attractive and successful owner of a thriving company. His days were usually hectic and filled with meetings and obligations, and he often worked overtime during the week. Yet I was always impressed with how truly present he was during our phone conversations. Though our exchanges were usually quite brief, he always showed an interest in how I was doing. I mean he showed a genuine interest, as opposed to what I would call a generic interest. Whenever I responded, I could tell he really heard me, based on his subsequent, specific comments.

The feedback I received about him was consistently glowing. The men I introduced Alex to always seemed to feel energized after meeting him. Even when some men didn't feel a potential dating or romantic chemistry with him, they expressed how they would like to develop a friendship.

I eventually introduced Alex to his current partner, Josh. Some of the matches I make just seem to be inevitable, and this was one of them. They currently live together. We check in with each other occasionally just to say hi, and they always seem to be doing quite well. I can also tell, even from our brief conversations, that Josh, a man who often seemed a bit brusque and ahead of himself initially, now appears to be more relaxed and in the moment. Yes, it's true—living in the now can be infectious.

He's Bad News!

Let's face it, guys: Not all Mr. Right candidates are as in-the-now-evolved as Alex, and it is important to notice the warning signs. Let's go back to your date. What are some of the indications that Mr. Man Across the Table might be, shall we say, not present in the present and thus less than future husband material?

Is he at all in the moment with you, or does he blab on and on about himself, never showing any interest in you, your life, or your thoughts? When you attempt to share information about yourself and what makes you tick, does he tune out, cruise the waiter, yawn, cruise the waiter, check his watch, cruise the waiter . . . you get the picture. Make sure you do get the picture!

If he's that uninterested in you now, what will he be like two, five, or ten years from now? Does your future happiness include that kind of inattention—that kind of jerk? You'd better believe it doesn't.

Here are some other clues that indicate a Not-in-the-Present Gent. As you listen to him, do you find him dishing his present life, and even his future life? Is he telling you—oh, let's just say it!—is he dumping on you just how rotten he thinks his life, or the world for that matter, currently is? Is he negatively predicting how it ain't going to get any better—based on his past experience? Do I need to say it? It would be a tough relationship road with this pessimistic, potential Prince Un-Charming.

If Those Aren't Enough, Here Are a Few More Clues . . .

Does he seem to be engaged in and jazzed about current aspects and interests in his life? Or does he continually recall the good ol' days of some time in his past while assuring you that life today truly sucks?

Does he exhibit immature or inappropriate behavior for a man his age? For example, is he a forty-year-old man behaving like a frat boy? (That may excite you as a fantasy, but be sure that's all it is!)

If, early on, he speaks only in the past tense and uses every opportunity during your conversation to tell yet another story from his college days or even farther back, that might indicate how little he values his life now.

If you find yourself in one of these situations, try steering the conversation to the present and see what he has to say. Yes, great stories from the past can be entertaining and enlightening once you get to know someone better but should not dominate your initial time together. It's most important to know who you're with now, not who he used to be.

Does he dress or wear his hair in a way that was distinctly popular five or ten years ago? Twenty or thirty years ago? Let's cut to the chase—is he wearing a Nehru jacket and sporting an Afro? Retro clothes and fashion can certainly be attractive and hot. Just figure out whether it's his fashion statement or his life statement.

These men often continue to dress and act the way they did when they felt they were at their best. Of course, this may simply indicate bad taste or lack of fashion savvy, but it can also mean that they're reluctant to consider new ideas and sensibilities. Just notice and decide how you feel about it.

OK, none of us are perfect. We all have our off-nights, none of us live in the now 24/7, and many of the points mentioned above are not necessarily Mr. Right deal breakers.

But if your good sense tells you that you are indeed with a sleazy character or someone you know you are incompatible with, find a diplomatic way to move the meeting along quickly, thank the guy for meeting you (just because you've decided he's all wrong for you and you can't get out of there fast enough, doesn't mean you have to be a jerk!), and leave with a smile and a handshake.

Who knows? If he's not a potential mate for you, maybe he'll become a friend who might later be the one to introduce you to Mr. Right. Strangely enough, I've seen that happen many times!

Mom and Dad

As gay men, Mom and Dad issues from the past—and in the present—are something we all deal with to differing degrees. I'm not a therapist, but based on numerous conversations with my clients and students, I have found that it's very difficult to have a thriving, full-fledged relationship if you have unsettled issues with either or both of your parents.

Some of you have, or have had, incredible relationships with your parents. Others have worked through a lot of Mom/Dad challenges and have developed great relationships, or at least have come out stronger within yourselves for your work. Congratulations! It makes your load that much lighter on the road to your own successful love relationship.

Others have not been as fortunate. Since we all know (or should know by now!) that we can't control the behavior of other people, usually the core Mom/Dad issue we're dealing with is one of forgiveness. Perhaps you haven't been able or willing to forgive them for things they may have done or may still be doing.

I know that forgiving a parent may not be easy, but here's the honest truth, guys, straight from the Gay Matchmaker: it is imperative to forgive past or ongoing hurts with your parents in order to flourish in a present love relationship.

Forgiving them doesn't mean that you condone their behavior, that you will necessarily have a close relationship with them, or that you actually forgive them in person. It just means that you've come to terms within yourself about what's happened between you in the past, you've accepted that reality in the present, and you've forgiven them for it. Only then can you stop reacting to their behavior, past and present, and move on.

Even if you haven't communicated directly with them or they've passed away, I strongly recommend you work through any parent issues that may be keeping you from a full-fledged relationship with another man.

If there was heavy-duty mental or physical abuse in your past, I encourage you to seek the help of a professional therapist to guide you through the process of forgiveness and healing. The process of working through Mom and Dad issues is ultimately about setting you free from restraining past influences.

It probably goes without saying, but I'll say it anyway. As you're working through challenges concerning your parents, seek ongoing support from close friends, other family members, a therapist, or a group designed for those issues, rather than a man you're just getting to know. If this man you've just recently met dominates your conversations with Mom/Dad issues, ask yourself if you're really ready for that.

Day 2 Weekly "Live in the Now" Exercises

When you're ready, take a few moments to consider—without judging yourself negatively—how successfully you live in the now. It's time to relieve yourself of that old baggage you might be carrying around, whether it's an overnight bag or an entire set, including the steamer trunk!

I describe baggage as any lingering pain, resentment, longing, or residual negative feelings from your past that might affect or color how you react today in a dating situation. Carrying around baggage can often force you into playing an old role from your past, such as "loser" or "victim" or "the perfect little boy" or "the one who always gets dumped" or whatever.

If your baggage consists mostly of not being able to let go of a past lover, you may find that you need more extensive help. I'd suggest reading the book *How to Survive the Loss of a Love* by Melba Colgrove, Harold H. Bloomfield, and Peter McWilliams. I've found the book most helpful in my own life and have passed it on to many others in need.

Here are some basic ways to help dump some of your baggage:

1. Put a label on your baggage—it's most important to know what you're dealing with. Is it your feelings about an old boyfriend?

Are you still angry with your parents? Did your past relationships cause you self-doubt or tremendous anxiety? Make a list of everything from your past that still affects you negatively today.

2. After each example, write down whether you felt you had any control over it at the time. If it was something you could control, then learn the lesson and use it to move forward. If you felt you had no control over what happened, consider the source of your old feelings. You might find that you were in no way at fault, so you have nothing to feel guilty or bad about.

3. Decide why you want to get rid of this old baggage. List what positive things could happen when you finally dump the old bags. Now, commit to moving forward. Write the commitment down as a promise to yourself, if that helps you move faster.

You may realize that you're in pretty good shape with some of these issues. If so, great! Take a moment to pat yourself on the back and then move on to the next. You needn't have all the answers—they may become apparent as you continue to appreciate being present in the moment.

Before you continue, pause a moment and take a few full, relaxing breaths. Close your eyes, if you like. Be still and simply be present.

Here are some additional questions to ask:

• When you're on a date, do you listen well?

Focus on listening today. This goes for everyone, but especially if you're a pro at dominating the conversation, turn the tables for a change and listen. After all, you already know you've got the gift of gab and can use that talent anytime you want. You might learn a heck of a lot about yourself—and another person—by stepping back and really hearing what others have to say. You might also be amazed at the additional amount of respect that comes your way.

- Based on your past experiences, do you tend to negatively predict how things will turn out, or do you stay present to create a positive experience?

  If you find yourself consistently predicting doom and gloom, take the active choice to stop this obnoxious "recording" in your head. Acknowledge the unwanted thought, then dismiss it by changing it—the same way you'd change an outgoing message on your cell phone! By changing the message, and you'll be amazed at how well you'll be received by others.

- Does your appearance/style place you in the past?

  I do not mean to say that you need to be a fashionista to be desirable, but dressing in the style of past decades (or even centuries) can indicate a fear of moving on. Up-to-date and age-appropriate hair and clothing styles tell potential dates that you live in the now. (Notice I said "age-appropriate." Let's stop fooling ourselves—and trying to fool others—by dressing in the past or trying to dress like someone twenty years younger than our own age.)

- Do you find yourself feeling resentful toward certain people? Do you live in regret over your own past actions?

  Time to forgive. Give yourself a few moments during the day to take a look at people you currently resent. Most importantly, this includes you! Decide that you forgive them for the day. If you're up to the challenge, imagine their lives working well for them. If they've passed away, wish them well. Notice how you feel at the end of the day.

- What are your other main challenges from the past regarding relationships? How are you taking steps to let go of each challenge? What are the negative patterns you've retained from childhood? How are you working through those patterns?

  It is important that you stop repeating the same failed behavior patterns from your past when you begin dating or starting a new relationship. Did you learn these patterns from your parents or even from other gay men in dysfunctional relationships? Have you heard that the definition of insanity is doing the same thing over and over and expecting different results? Well, it's true. Only you really know your own past challenges. It's time for you to be honest and clear about identifying and releasing these patterns. It's never too late to learn a better way.

Day 2 each week is also about paring down and letting go. You're making room for new and now energy and possessions in your life. Go through your closets, desks, and drawers and throw out, give to charity, or pass along to a friend any extraneous possessions you haven't used or worn in the past year. It's a freeing experience that will literally dispense with the past and make room for the new. After you've completed a major paring down, continue each week to choose three to five possessions (books, magazines, knickknacks, CDs, videos, articles of clothing, etc.) to throw out or give away to a friend or charitable organization. Then do it. It's also a great day to organize closets, files, drawers, the attic, the basement, the garage, the glove compartment and trunk of your car, or cupboards that have fallen into disarray.

During Day 2 of this Plan, you'll discover how living in the now will bring great rewards not only to your dating life, but also to your life overall. It is impossible to fully connect with a date or partner if you continue to be a prisoner of the past. You may be able to share common past experiences, but you won't discover many unique and spontaneous moments.

So, take a deep breath and show the past the door. It's time to finally let go and create the space to redesign and make over the present—the *now!*

DAY 3

Open Up *and* Extend

"Overall, I'm comfortable in my life, and I don't feel motivated or excited when it comes to looking for a boyfriend. A partner might be nice, but guys I meet never live up to my standards. I'm always disappointed. It's just the way I am."
—Ramon Rigid

"I haven't dated for over three years and don't really know if I want to. I mean, I've seen it all in the dating scene and it's not for me. The men out there are tired! Been there, done that, got the T-shirt... OVER IT!"
—Arthur Apathy

Well, guys, here they are! Meet the Un–Dynamic Duo . . . Ramon Rigid and Arthur Apathy!!! (Applause. Bows. Curtain.) . . . That's right, Curtain. They've already squelched any possibility of dating success, let alone relationship success.

Which scintillating guy should we meet first? Oh, what the hell, let's start with Mr. Rigid.

Ramon

During my initial meeting with thirty-two-year-old designer Ramon Rigid, I quickly realized I was dealing with a man who was entirely caught up in his own orbit, partially due to all sorts of pressures from his fast-paced life. As creative, open and successful as he clearly was in his fashion career, he seemed totally closed to any new ideas about dating or finding a relationship.

When I first spoke to him on the phone, his tone was almost completely lifeless. To say he was blasé would be an understatement. Frankly, I was surprised he actually came to the appointment he made to meet me. But, surprise! He did deign to grace my office with his presence.

I must tell you, I did my utmost to get Ramon to approach dating in a new, fun, and creative way. But he remained as steadfast as a nun during Lent. Having strong opinions is one thing. Ramon was completely unyielding and closed off to virtually all my suggestions and ideas.

Essentially, he was refusing to venture outside his own orbit of actions and beliefs by refuting any other point of view. As a result, the feedback I received about him from his introductions was consistently negative.

My clients and workshop students can sometimes get caught up in this closed way of thinking. They frequently use words like "always" and "never." They can be rigid in their resolve, perhaps fearing that any unknown might pierce their perfectly calculated lives.

I always feel a little sad when I see these tendencies in those with whom I work. It really makes it difficult for them to appreciate any uniqueness or freshness in another person. They may feel safe on some level in their comfort zone of absolutes. But fearing to venture outside that zone ultimately limits the dating and relationship opportunities that could await them.

Arthur

OK, my meeting with Mr. Arthur Apathy, age forty-one, brings me to a subject that's huge!

When I'm first speaking to a client about himself, I always ask him what he feels are the strongest attributes or characteristics he would bring to a potential relationship. When I posed this question to Arthur, he immediately rattled off an extensive list of all the qualities his date or partner must possess. He didn't disclose a single, positive, personal quality that he himself might bring to a date.

I found this very telling. Like many single men tend to do, he only thought in terms of assessing the other guy, with little consideration of what he himself had to offer. To a date, this unwillingness to extend can, indeed, come off as apathy—and downright unappealing!

Ironically, when Arthur first came through the door of my office, warmly extended his hand, and shook mine, I remember a basic feeling of hopefulness and potential for him. Within minutes, through his continual negativity, that hopefulness and potential pretty much evaporated.

I truly hate to see these people sabotage themselves and their dating possibilities, all in the name of being right. I've long ago lost count of the times I've encountered "you can't show me anything new" people. They are so insistent on negatively predicting outcomes. Their gloom-and-doom attitude makes me want to shout, "Lighten up!"

These apathetic types tend to construct scenarios of what they're certain will happen. They have an immovable outlook and set of criteria and are not willing to extend themselves beyond their jaded expectations, having decided that it would be futile. "What's the point?" often becomes their mantra.

Why do some guys behave this way? I imagine it keeps their fear of imperfection, disappointment, and failure at bay. It's also a sure way to alienate those who are willing to extend.

In essence, the Ramon Rigids and Arthur Apathys of this world have never developed the simple but significant art of "extending."

"Love isn't something you feel, but something
   you do"
                              —Author unknown

Kip and Elliot

When Kip walked into my office about six years ago, my first thought was, "Well, what do you know—Clark Kent in the flesh!"

Kip was an attractive, reserved, Ivy League–educated twenty-eight-year-old CPA with a major accounting firm. He was fairly shy, with an earnest and precise manner. But the trait that endeared him most to me was his honesty.

Early on in our interview, as he opened up to me about himself, he admitted, "I give new meaning to the words 'anal retentive'!" He then somewhat sheepishly revealed how obsessive he was about having everything—and I do mean everything—in its proper place. I was literally struck dumb as he described his day-to-day life. From the precise and immaculate layout of all of the material possessions in his apartment, through every aspect of his daily routine, he maintained a need for total order, structure, and control.

Not surprisingly, he also revealed to me that, sexually, he thought of himself as a total top in all respects.

Kip admitted he'd never had a relationship with a man that lasted beyond a few weeks. When we started to discuss the sorts of men he was most interested in meeting, he seemed to have a one-track mind—namely, men similar to himself. As he put it, "Who else could put up with me, but someone just like me?" I was in no way convinced of that but decided to acquiesce to his wishes, at least at the beginning.

The first three men I introduced to Kip to were, indeed, similar to him. Each candidate was close in age, each had a business career, and, though perhaps not to Kip's extreme, each guy was fairly ordered, structured, and rigid in personality and lifestyle. After the meeting with Businessman Bachelor number three, Kip asked to stop by my office for a chat.

As he described the basic chemistry he felt with each of his three introductions, Kip mentioned how he did find them all attractive and pleasant. Then he replied, "But isn't dating supposed to be fun? With each of these guys, I felt like I was still at the office!" A-ha! A breakthrough!

Kip then admitted that the main reason that he had originally come to work with me was to break out of the restricting patterns in his life. I asked Kip if he was willing to trust me and, perhaps, shake things up a bit. After a brief hesitation and fleeting look of concern, he replied, "I guess it is time to risk a bit."

We went in a new direction with Kip's contacts. I introduced him to a series of men with very diverse interests and personality traits. Throughout the process, I kept saying to him, "Stay open and just remember to look at these meetings as new adventures."

I gotta hand it to Kip. For what appeared to be the first time in his life, he truly embraced the unknown. He really did roll with the punches, and gradually he began to revel in the whole process.

At one point I remembered Kip telling me that he went through a period in adolescence when he had pursued acting. Seeing my surprise at the time, he quipped, "I'd really enjoyed it. I actually got some very positive feedback!" I decided to introduce him to Elliot.

A thirty-one-year-old casting director, Elliot was a boyish, upbeat man. He was warm, funny, and spontaneous. As far as extending goes, let's just say that I've rarely come across a man as giving and generous of heart as Elliot.

Though they were two very different sorts of men, there turned out to be an immediate and definite spark between them. As he and Kip began to date, Elliot clearly enjoyed the differences between them—and so did Kip. He even began to re-explore a shelved interest in acting by taking some classes.

Months went by, and their relationship deepened. One night I ran into Kip and Elliot at a gay fund-raiser. Elliot seemed quite happy, and I couldn't help but notice the change in Kip. He seemed so much more relaxed and secure within himself than the man I remembered from months before.

When Elliott went off to pick up drinks, I mentioned that to Kip, and he replied, "Yeah, it's pretty amazing how this relationship has opened me up." He then added, with a sly grin, "I've definitely gotten more in touch with my 'inner bottom!'"

Kip and Elliot are still together today, living on the West Coast. Every once in a while I get a postcard or a phone call. I couldn't be happier for them.

Day 3 Weekly "Open Up and Extend" Exercises

Extending is one of the most significant principles of any relationship at all levels. On Day 3, focus on this one basic truth—that the positive aspects of our lives emanate from the simple choice we make to extend and maximize the best of ourselves.

We all have orbits we live in. Daily patterns in our lives can make us feel safe and comfortable. Before you focus on ways you can open up or extend more, take a bit of time to acknowledge the areas of your daily life that are already working well—areas where you feel open and extending. They can be in any aspect of your life—friendships, work, money, or appearance. I'll help you start the Day 3 exercises by providing a place to make a list. Just as you did in for the Day 1 exercise—grab a pencil—and feel free to extend the list!

"Things That Already Work in My Orbit" List

1. _____

2. _____

3. _____

4. _____

5. _____

This list can be a great reminder of some ways that you have already created a foundation in your life. I'll be the first to say that feeling secure and comfortable is important, but sometimes we get too comfortable. How do you know if your comfort zone is getting a bit too cozy? Ask yourself these questions:

- Does your work life, or your love life, fill you with a sense of excitement or possibility?

- Do you feel passionate about your daily actions, or are you simply in an apathetic orbit?

- Are you paralyzed by the idea of a new way of thinking or approaching someone?

If you answered "yes" to any of these questions, you may be in something of a rut.

Many of the clients and students I've worked with through the years are scared to death of going outside their safe orbit in any way that might make a difference. In order for them to open up and expand their dating/relationship potential and to work through the fear that comes up with risking new behavior or possibilities, I have them make a "risk list." It's not as scary as it sounds.

Let's start with some simple risks. They can include activities outside your normal arena, making time for people you usually don't, learning about things you've previously had no knowledge of, or driving a different way to a destination.

Five Simple Risks I Could Take to Open Up

1. _____

2. _____

3. _____

4. _____

5. _____

Now, give yourself permission to take these small risks. You're not uprooting your entire existence by doing something radical! You're expanding or "tweaking" your comfort zone gradually and with confidence. Your "been there, done that" or "I just don't give a damn" attitude may just gradually change to one of renewed passion. What's more attractive than that?

The Larger Sense . . .

Making a risk list is a great way to start opening up. Perhaps you've decided to learn a new language. Great! Not only will you become more knowledgeable, but you'll now have another way to extend to people you may not have even acknowledged before. In no time, you'll find how well taking small risks pays off.

Perhaps your inability or refusal to open up or extend comes from a much deeper place. Maybe you've been rigid or apathetic for so long that taking even simple risks seems impossible or absurd to you. It's been my observation that many people become rigid or apathetic because they've lost touch with their passions, their sense of humor, or even their hopes and dreams.

Let's make a different type of list. Because this list may be deeply personal, go ahead and make it on a separate sheet of paper or in a private journal. But, definitely make this list. As I said before, list making is very often the first action of change. Ask yourself the following questions and list the answers:

Presently, what brings you the greatest satisfaction? Has it changed in the past five years or so? If so, in what ways? Have these changes been for the better or have they manifested in feelings of apathy? What actions can you now take to bring more satisfaction into your life? Answering these questions will help you to expel negative, jaded feelings.

How would you describe your sense of humor? How have others described it? If you've lost yours, list some ways to start laughing again. A great sense of humor is so attractive to others. What makes you laugh? Do you laugh as much as you used to? If not, why not? Then, bring your sense of humor along with you on your next date.

What makes you emotional? Our emotions are the most immediate way in which we extend. If you find you are feeling emotionless, ask yourself what used to make you emotional. If you are avoiding emotional subjects, you may be trying to avoid pain. But, you're also avoiding joy. Of course, we all express our emotions differently and in varying degrees, but one thing's for certain—it's difficult to love a cold fish.

What issues do you care most about? Where does your greatest empathy lie? How are you currently paying attention to these areas? Extending in areas where you feel most empathetic can bring an intense feeling of satisfaction and self-worth. Apathy cannot exist where passion and empathy thrive.

Passion, empathy, and humor are wonderful qualities to bring when meeting a date or potential partner. By opening up and extending, you'll find ways to rediscover the joy of developing relationships where both people reach out to present their best, while focusing on each other.

"Our passions are ourselves."
—Author unknown

DAY 4

Balance

"I'm so into my career. I'd call myself a 'professional human being and a kick-ass-multi-tasker.' I'm very structured and busy and I have no free time. I'm an actor, a singer, a musician and I work at Tele-charge during the day and then I'm a go-go-dancer in the evening and then I perform in my own late-night cabaret and then . . . Who the hell has the time to go on a real date?"

—Bobby BusyBusy

Valium, anyone? Like my previous assistant, Bobby BusyBusy, many of us (including yours truly) jam-pack our schedules these days. This is the most prevalent challenge that I encounter with clients regarding effective dating.

A large percentage of single gay men are heavily focused on super-sizing their careers, making lots of money, or just surviving in these tougher economic times. So they develop a myopic career mindset as a substitute for making a meaningful connection with another man. Because these workaholics may fear giving up control (God forbid!)

and revealing a more vulnerable side of themselves, they often respond by going nose-to-the-grindstone at their jobs or over-scheduling their lives in general. Their schedule is something they can control, but it leaves them little time to include a potential Main Man in the balance.

Let's look at a few other examples of dating sabotaged because a guy's life balance is out of whack.

Irving Image

Two summers ago, when Irving Image came to my office for a dating coaching session, my first impression was, "Wow! This man looks phenomenal!"

A fifty-four-year-old event planner, Irving had a hard sculpted body, a deep bronze tan, a set of dazzling white teeth, and a perfectly chiseled face. It was very obvious (and impressive!) that Irving spent a lot of his time cultivating and maintaining "the look."

When we began to discuss what was currently going on in his life, it seemed to be pretty much along one track. Irving had just started workouts with his third new trainer in six months. He knew the new blond highlights in his hair were too much, but Flash, his current hairdresser, would take care of that later this week. He also confided, as he lowered his voice, that he had just discovered the most incredible plastic surgeon, new to town from LA.

Irving went on to mention that, although he'd basically been comfortable with his sexuality since his teens, he had never had an ongoing relationship with a man that had lasted beyond six weeks. His two most recently ended involvements, three weeks each, were with a twenty-nine-year-old makeup artist and a thirty-three-year-old personal trainer. Although the sex was very hot, after a short time with each of them, he said, there just wasn't much to talk about.

I noticed a similar problem between Irving and me as we continued to chat. After discussing his dedication to his face and body, the rest of my inquiries about his life were basically met with general, curt replies. Irving appeared to have a distinct lack of interest in hobbies, culture, politics, spirituality, his family, or even his friends. Overall, he seemed emotionally detached and limited to conversations about physicality. This could take him only so far on a date. My work was cut out for me!

Seth Self-Help

About seven or eight years ago, I was doing one of my seasonal, all-day workshops at the Gay and Lesbian Community Center. We had just finished for the day, and I was chatting with some of the guys as they were leaving and wishing them good luck.

Seth, a twenty-six-year-old man who had participated, approached me with a wide-eyed grin. "This day was so amazing for me!" he exclaimed. "I felt like I really got in touch with a lot of my stuff—like, dating baggage and everything—and I'd really like to talk to you about it. Do you have time to grab a cup of coffee?" After my workshops I tend to feel especially energized and empathetic with my students. A cup of coffee? Sure—why not?

Two and a half hours later, I could write you a full resume of Seth's journey during the past three years through the worlds of self-help, human potential, and spirituality. This trek included completing all the levels of the Lifespring and Forum seminars, sampling every New Age and New Thought church in the area, going on countless weekend retreats and, currently, attending regular meetings for Alcoholics Anonymous, Narcotics Anonymous, and Sexual Compulsives Anonymous.

As obsessive as this may sound, I'm not exaggerating! I remember thinking to myself, "Is there a twelve-step meeting for twelve-step addicts?" I had to wonder if Seth put the same amount of dedication and energy into his career, his physical health, or his other pursuits. It didn't sound like it to me.

Drew Drama

It was early fall two years ago, when Drew Drama, a thirty-six-year-old dancer-choreographer, came in to the ManMate office to sign up for our Dinners for 8 membership. When I asked him what had recently been happening in his life in terms of meeting new men, a better question might have been, what wasn't happening?

Drew was loaded with stories of entanglements and intrigue from his just-completed season of summer stock . . . and he seemed to be at the center of all of them! Drew was the resident choreographer for a summer theater company in Michigan, which opened a new musical every week for twelve weeks. Jobbed-in actors, singers, and dancers were zipping in and out of town throughout the summer, and, apparently, chorus boys were zipping in and out of his bedroom all season as well.

I have to admit that my assistant, Michael, and I listened with rapt attention. A born storyteller, Drew was riveting, as he careened from one show's dalliance to the next. Pretty soon, though, the Chads and Kyles and Jasons all ran together, and I completely lost track.

What was most amazing, though, was how much stock (no pun intended) Drew seemed to put into each of these brief encounters. As he passionately recalled each involvement, it was as if he was reliving all the emotions he had apparently gone through with each man. By the end of his summer stock saga, a misty-eyed Drew concluded that he had indeed fallen in love . . . with three different men!

So why, I asked, was he looking to complicate matters by meeting a slew of new, single men at a series of dinner parties? Wouldn't it get, oh, I don't know, confusing? "Not at all," Drew replied. "I've moved on."

Where Are They Now?

So what happened to this trio of balance-challenged gents?

Irving, still single but a bit less image-obsessed, relocated to South Beach last year.

Drew was a hit at the dinner parties and recently started dating a fellow dining partner . . . someone *not* working in theater! It actually looks promising.

A while back I introduced Seth, who started working with me after that all-day workshop, to Jonathan, a twenty-nine-year-old social worker. Seth became a teacher, and they've been happily living together in a quiet suburb for the past five years.

This is why I do what I do.

The Balancing Act

So, how do you achieve a balance that works well in your life and makes you a more desirable date? Let's get real . . . there is no absolute balancing act a guy can adopt to integrate dating perfectly into his life. There can, however, be some basic guidelines.

To have a chance at a full-fledged relationship, it really is essential to explore the varied aspects of life and to give attention to each important area—physical, mental, emotional, and spiritual.

Your physical life refers to anything pertaining to the activities and health of your body.

Your mental life consists of your thoughts, knowledge, work, schedule, and all things organizational and left-brained.

Your full range of feelings and creativity composes your emotional life.

Your spiritual life refers to those areas that affect your spirit or soul or whatever you choose to call it. Spirituality may or may not include religious beliefs, but certainly reflects your own belief system, values, and opinions. Your spirituality is that which affirms you.

Day 4 Weekly "Balance" Exercises

The following are a series of statements to help you determine if any area(s) of your life are being overemphasized to the exclusion of others. Some statements could refer to more than one area. Again, there is no perfect balancing act. This is to help you decide how the scales tip in your life.

Respond to each statement by checking one of the following (remember to write in pencil so you can later change your responses as you begin to find better balance in your life):

❑ Usually
❑ Often
❑ Sometimes
❑ Rarely

Physical
I eat a healthy, balanced diet.
❑ Usually
❑ Often
❑ Sometimes
❑ Rarely

I get at least six to eight hours of uninterrupted sleep a night.
❑ Usually
❑ Often
❑ Sometimes
❑ Rarely

I exercise at least three times a week.
❑ Usually
❑ Often
❑ Sometimes
❑ Rarely

I go for routine health care checkups and physicals.
- ❑ Usually
- ❑ Often
- ❑ Sometimes
- ❑ Rarely

I have a flattering wardrobe that I enjoy wearing.
- ❑ Usually
- ❑ Often
- ❑ Sometimes
- ❑ Rarely

I am at a healthy weight.
- ❑ Usually
- ❑ Often
- ❑ Sometimes
- ❑ Rarely

I enjoy sex and have a fulfilling sex life.
- ❑ Usually
- ❑ Often
- ❑ Sometimes
- ❑ Rarely

I am content with the way I look.
- ❑ Usually
- ❑ Often
- ❑ Sometimes
- ❑ Rarely

I need to smoke to keep going.
- ❑ Usually
- ❑ Often
- ❑ Sometimes
- ❑ Rarely

I need caffeine to keep going.
❑ Usually
❑ Often
❑ Sometimes
❑ Rarely

I am comfortable with my alcohol intake.
❑ Usually
❑ Often
❑ Sometimes
❑ Rarely

I seek out health-conscious friends and dates.
❑ Usually
❑ Often
❑ Sometimes
❑ Rarely

Spiritual

I have strong beliefs that help me through rough times.
❑ Usually
❑ Often
❑ Sometimes
❑ Rarely

I have a small group of confidants I can talk to when things get tough.
❑ Usually
❑ Often
❑ Sometimes
❑ Rarely

I make time to be a confidant to others.
- ❏ Usually
- ❏ Often
- ❏ Sometimes
- ❏ Rarely

I take time out during the day for me.
- ❏ Usually
- ❏ Often
- ❏ Sometimes
- ❏ Rarely

I maintain a positive outlook on life.
- ❏ Usually
- ❏ Often
- ❏ Sometimes
- ❏ Rarely

I spend time developing my creative gifts and interests.
- ❏ Usually
- ❏ Often
- ❏ Sometimes
- ❏ Rarely

I feel anxious about my place in the world.
- ❏ Usually
- ❏ Often
- ❏ Sometimes
- ❏ Rarely

I take time to enjoy and celebrate accomplishments.
- ❏ Usually
- ❏ Often
- ❏ Sometimes
- ❏ Rarely

I take active steps to alleviate stress.
❑ Usually
❑ Often
❑ Sometimes
❑ Rarely

I take time to remind myself of what makes me happy.
❑ Usually
❑ Often
❑ Sometimes
❑ Rarely

I take time to consider other philosophies and points of view.
❑ Usually
❑ Often
❑ Sometimes
❑ Rarely

I seek out life-affirming friends and dates.
❑ Usually
❑ Often
❑ Sometimes
❑ Rarely

Emotional

I work on ways to deal with my anger.
❑ Usually
❑ Often
❑ Sometimes
❑ Rarely

I keep in touch with friends to avoid becoming lonely.
- ❑ Usually
- ❑ Often
- ❑ Sometimes
- ❑ Rarely

I take steps when dealing with depression.
- ❑ Usually
- ❑ Often
- ❑ Sometimes
- ❑ Rarely

I find it easy to express emotions.
- ❑ Usually
- ❑ Often
- ❑ Sometimes
- ❑ Rarely

I take the time to breathe when I start to feel emotionally overwhelmed.
- ❑ Usually
- ❑ Often
- ❑ Sometimes
- ❑ Rarely

I am honest with myself about my emotions.
- ❑ Usually
- ❑ Often
- ❑ Sometimes
- ❑ Rarely

I am honest with my friends, family, and dates about my emotions.
❑ Usually
❑ Often
❑ Sometimes
❑ Rarely

I have been referred to as a "drama queen."
❑ Usually
❑ Often
❑ Sometimes
❑ Rarely

I deny my emotions.
❑ Usually
❑ Often
❑ Sometimes
❑ Rarely

I bask in my emotions.
❑ Usually
❑ Often
❑ Sometimes
❑ Rarely

I find myself feeling empty and void of emotion.
❑ Usually
❑ Often
❑ Sometimes
❑ Rarely

I seek out emotionally mature and accessible friends and dates.
- ❏ Usually
- ❏ Often
- ❏ Sometimes
- ❏ Rarely

Mental

I organize my time effectively.
- ❏ Usually
- ❏ Often
- ❏ Sometimes
- ❏ Rarely

I fall behind schedule.
- ❏ Usually
- ❏ Often
- ❏ Sometimes
- ❏ Rarely

I beat myself up mentally.
- ❏ Usually
- ❏ Often
- ❏ Sometimes
- ❏ Rarely

I'm a workaholic.
- ❏ Usually
- ❏ Often
- ❏ Sometimes
- ❏ Rarely

I do at least two fun activities that I enjoy every week.
- ❑ Usually
- ❑ Often
- ❑ Sometimes
- ❑ Rarely

I attend social functions.
- ❑ Usually
- ❑ Often
- ❑ Sometimes
- ❑ Rarely

I take steps to make sure that I am financially sound.
- ❑ Usually
- ❑ Often
- ❑ Sometimes
- ❑ Rarely

I plan for the future.
- ❑ Usually
- ❑ Often
- ❑ Sometimes
- ❑ Rarely

I dwell on the past and what I missed out on.
- ❑ Usually
- ❑ Often
- ❑ Sometimes
- ❑ Rarely

I live in the present by staying in the moment.
- ❑ Usually
- ❑ Often
- ❑ Sometimes
- ❑ Rarely

I find time to keep developing my mind by learning new things.
- ❑ Usually
- ❑ Often
- ❑ Sometimes
- ❑ Rarely

I seek out mentally stimulating friends and dates.
- ❑ Usually
- ❑ Often
- ❑ Sometimes
- ❑ Rarely

Excellent! Now just take an overall look at how you responded to each section.

Was there a section or sections in which your answers were more immediate and more certain? Did you feel uncertain in any of the sections? By first taking an overall look at the balance of your answers, you can notice where you might be short-changing some areas or challenges in your life. Then, by taking a closer look at certain responses, you'll be able to see where greater challenges might lie.

Sometimes, just tweaking your focus in little ways can help with your balance challenges immensely. For example, if your schedule is out of control, or you currently overemphasize the mental aspects of your life, simple actions like taking time to breathe, making eye contact, actually stopping to listen, and knowing when to turn off the cell phone can make a difference.

Who knows? If your schedule is always in overdrive, you may be blindly rushing right past some key dating potential that's right in front of you.

If you're the type of person that needs a stronger incentive, then I'd I encourage you to make a "contract" with yourself. This contract could state that you will begin to reprioritize your goals to give equal and fair attention to all areas of your life—including friendships and family.

Let me say again that there is no definite formula for perfect balance for the dating seesaw that I know of, but, after twenty-two years of matchmaking, I have seen many potential dates fizzle out due to a pronounced imbalance in the life of one or both of the guys involved. By becoming a more balanced individual, you'll not only be a more interesting date, but you'll also find more day-to-day clarity, which is crucial to the growth of any relationship.

DAY 5

Be Patient, Responsible, *and* Respectful

"He's got a butt that could stop a war! I'm sorry,
but I've gotta find out how hot he is in bed. Then
I'll think about dating him."
—Sammy SexMachine

Let's see, when did I meet Sammy SexMachine? Oh, about ten thousand times or so—there are many different versions of him on any given night in every gay bar and club in the world!

Sammy SexMachine is that hot-to-trot guy in need of instant gratification. He has a libido that often overcomes, even overwhelms, his sense of reason. The choices a Sammy SexMachine makes aren't based on possible dating potential, but rather on the narrow path of his urgent sexual needs. Like an impatient child, he wants it *now*!

Sammy SexMachine fears that he may lose an exciting, sexual opportunity if he doesn't seize it immediately! So because he hasn't developed the confidence necessary to be patient, his romantic life can turn into little more than an addiction to one-night stands and booty calls.

We've all been there. We've all succumbed to our immediate sexual urges for a guy at one time or another. I'm not making a judgment about it; I'm just reminding us all that quickly getting off with a virtual stranger doesn't usually lead to dating magic!

Be Patient

Sex changes things. I'm not saying it's *never* going to work out in the long run with a partner you have sex with on the first date. But let's face it. Doesn't the excitement of discovering things about your date (such as his last name!) seem a bit anticlimactic or less thrilling after you've spent a night doing the most intimate physical things imaginable? You've heard that old cliché, "the joy in savoring the main course can lessen after you've already had the dessert"? It's a cliché for a reason. How interested will you be in finding out more about your date (like that tendency he has to lie, or that drinking problem, or his real age, or the fact that he still lives with Mom or . . . get my point?) when you've already spent the night tongue bathing each other and now you can't live without him?

So, when should you have sex with someone you've just started seeing? There have been so many theories written about this—two dates . . . three dates . . . five dates . . . twenty dates! There is no definitive number.

My feeling has always been that sex should happen when both men have at least gotten to know the basics about one another and respect each other as human and sexual beings. Only you and your date will know when that time comes. If you still feel that having sex with a date immediately is what you require, then enjoy and hope for the best!

I've seen firsthand that it is, indeed, often more difficult to go back and attempt to form a foundation for a potential relationship when you've "gotten it on" early on. When we start a membership at Man-Mate, one of the main guidelines we give for first dates has always been, "Meet in a neutral place, outside your home or apartment."

First dates are all about getting to know each other. How do your personalities mesh? Where are you both in your lives? What interests and values do you share? Are you really physically attracted to each other or just horny?

I can't tell you the number of stories I've heard through the years from men who were attracted to a promising Mr. Right, jumped into bed right away, and, sizzling though the sex may have been, found that it was their first, and only, "date." It surprises me when they're surprised!

There's a reason why patience has been called a virtue. The confidence to be patient can make love, dating, and relationships that much more meaningful, even exciting. It also allows a man the space to get to know a potential partner better, making sex that much hotter when the time is right.

Playing Victim

> "What can I say? All men are pigs!"
> —Victor Victim

When Victor Victim stepped into my office recently, he was full of stories of all the men who'd done him wrong. He was a walking torch singer. As far as the four six-month relationships he had had during the past three years, he'd basically washed his hands of any responsibility for their outcomes.

I think he'd already decided I wouldn't be able to introduce him effectively. Guess what? He's probably going to be right. He has yet to get that, ultimately, he is steering the wheel toward his dating/relationship destiny.

The Victor Victims we all know don't want to take real responsibility for their actions in relationships—leaving a hell of a lot of extra work for the rest of us! The victim mentality can be very tempting because it provides the opportunity to assign blame elsewhere.

How often do we hear, "Men are pigs!" or "I never get a break"? The men behind these declarations continually put themselves in the position of merely reacting to others and blaming them, instead of taking any responsibility for their actions.

Entitled to Be the Victim?

Edward Entitled, thirty-five, sat across from me and proclaimed that many people in his life mistreated him, and he had really had his fill of it all. He asked if there was any chance that I could find someone for him who wasn't "an asshole." I assured him there was, but at the same time had to wonder why he came off as such a victim. So I asked him some general questions about his life.

Edward had just been passed over for a promotion at his office. I inquired if he knew what the reason might be. He said, "My jerk of a boss hates me and is out to get me. That promotion was mine!" When I pressed further and asked if he had talked with his boss, Edward then said, "Oh yeah . . . and he made up some crap about performance reports or whatever . . . but I know the real reason." I then asked if he felt supported enough by his co-workers to get their input. "They're jealous of me because I get my work done faster than they do and can usually leave earlier."

When we finally got around to discussing his last, failed relationship, it was more of the same. He was quick to blame his ex-lover and again cast himself in the victim role. A pattern began to emerge: Edward saw his problems as a result of everyone else's behavior and didn't get how he might be culpable in any way.

I won't even pretend to have the answer for why he behaves this way. That's a whole different book! What I have noticed is that I'm meeting more and more men who have adopted an "I'm entitled" attitude. They expect all the best to come to them without having to be responsible for any part of its success or failure. On some level, they feel things should just fall into their laps and claim victimization when they don't. I think it's clear to see how this attitude can sabotage a dating life.

My feeling is that we're really not entitled to anything we haven't put effort and a sense of responsibility toward—including successful relationships.

Perhaps when you were young, you heard what many other children hear from parents. Mom and Dad might have said, "Nothing's good enough for our boy." That doesn't translate into "You should have everything you want handed to you without any responsibility attached."

You may have also heard, "No one's good enough for our boy." That doesn't translate into "See, I am better than other guys and shouldn't be held accountable. They have to live up to me—the world owes *me!*"

Of course these statements, as damaging as they are if believed literally, were intended to show how much your parents love you and want the best for you. Yet the statements "nothing's good enough" or "no one's good enough" never lead to satisfaction for the recipient.

If you believe that nothing or no one's good enough for you, then ultimately you're buying into a life of disillusionment. This belief is also an open invitation to the victim mentality.

They Can't Read Your Mind

As soon as I heard his voice on the phone, I knew I should have screened my calls. For the third time that week, Patrick was on the other end, more distraught than usual. I had introduced him to Brian a few months earlier, and the two had become an item. But now, there seemed to be trouble in paradise.

According to Patrick, Brian could do nothing right and continued to disappoint and hurt Patrick at every turn. Patrick claimed Brian was insensitive to his needs. No matter how many nice things Patrick did for him, Brian never responded the way Patrick wanted. According to Patrick, Brian just didn't get it and didn't care how much he was hurting. Patrick was tired of being devastated.

My next simple question silenced and seemed to floor Patrick. I asked, "Have you told him what you need and expect?" After a lengthy pause, Patrick responded, "Why should I have to do that? He should be sensitive enough to just know. . . . I do."

"It sounds like you expect Brian to be a mind reader," I replied.

"That's ridiculous," exclaimed Patrick, as he hung up in a snit.

At the time, I felt I may have been too blunt, but it seemed unfair to hold Brian completely accountable when Patrick wasn't verbally communicating to him how he felt.

Patrick called me back the next day. He had given our conversation some thought and planned to begin verbally expressing his needs to Brian.

It doesn't always work out this well. I'm glad it did this time. One less victim in the world . . .

> **"A lot of people are afraid to say what they want.**
> **That's why they don't get what they want."**
> **—Madonna**

Be Responsible

To date successfully or to have a healthy relationship that works for both men, it is essential that both claim responsibility for successes and failures. It's just too easy to be in reaction and blame the other guy for everything.

Of course, it's possible to truly be the victim of someone else's behavior. We've all been true victims from time to time. Shit happens. But it's important to know when we share responsibility and when we don't.

Playing the victim may seem to pay off in the minds of certain men, but the truth is, there is no power in being the victim.

Reliability, Pure and Simple

> "Look, I was only a half hour late and he gave
> me such attitude—what's up with that? I'm very
> busy and he's really not my type anyway."
> —Ulysses Unreliable

The one complaint I get more than any other about dating refers to guys like Ulysses Unreliable. We all know the type. He promises to call—and then doesn't. He constantly shows up late—or not at all. He leads you on—and then dumps you. He makes a date with you—as a last resort. Wrong on so many levels!

Men like this tend to be very concerned about protecting their own agenda and feelings, with little regard or respect for another's. Sometimes, unfortunately, you just don't see it coming.

Jeremy

Almost a year ago, Jeremy contacted me to meet and start a ManMate membership "ASAP." It sounded serious! We met later that night.

When Jeremy walked into my office, he had charisma written all over him. A stunningly attractive, thirty-seven-year-old, well-built, high-powered attorney, Jeremy looked to be the sort of man just about any single gay guy could fall for . . . at first sight.

As we discussed what was happening in his life, I have to say the man was mesmerizing. Here was an engaging, passionate guy with a terrific sense of humor. He clearly approached every aspect of his life, from his demanding law practice to his daily, strenuous workouts, with energized gusto. Now, he confided to me, "I'm ready to find the right guy and make a relationship work."

Jeremy was interested in shifting his dating life into high gear immediately. His sense of urgency was infectious, and I have to admit I got swept up in his enthusiasm.

Within a few weeks' time, I had introduced Jeremy to three candidates. Each man was initially interested in getting to know him better, and the feeling was mutual. What could be more promising?

During the next month, Jeremy continued to juggle dates with all three guys. Although this approach might be overwhelming and un-workable for many gay men, I don't necessarily find it objectionable. At this early stage, there usually isn't an implied exclusivity between two guys, and some men want to get a perspective on what feels like real dating potential.

At the same time, it clearly works better for many guys to get to know one man at a time. What can I say? It depends on the guy.

Jeremy seemed to be maximizing his dating potential. He very diligently and positively kept me posted on his progress, and each of the three men was pretty much equally enthusiastic.

Then a strange thing happened: Jeremy disappeared.

Within a couple of days, I received calls from three confused men. All of them were perplexed. Each of their last dates with Jeremy had gone well, and then suddenly he stopped returning their calls and e-mails. So over the next few days, I myself left an e-mail and a phone message for him and didn't hear back. Jeremy had dropped off the face of the earth.

Three weeks went by. One afternoon, I picked up the office phone. Guess who?

"Grant! I am so sorry I haven't gotten back to you! I have been swamped! I'm afraid I haven't even had a moment to get back to Tom, Ted, or Tyrone! I've barely had time to fit in my daily work-outs! I'm not a guy who drops the ball like this, but my schedule's been crazy!"

Jeremy continued apologizing for another couple of minutes. So I did what any sane gay matchmaker would do: I called him into my office, turned him over my knee and spanked him . . . Just kidding! But I'm amazed at how a successful professional guy, seemingly mature on all levels, can have the follow-through and basic courtesy skills in his personal life of a self-centered adolescent boy.

"I Know, I Know! You're So Busy and Important!"

I know all about busy. You see, I live in frenetic New York City. But, no matter where you live in these busy times, I'm sure you've met the "I'm so busy and important" type like Jeremy. OK, so men like Jeremy are very busy and feel they have very important jobs. And those biceps are not going to balloon up by themselves!

But guess what? We're all busy and important and value our time. That doesn't give anyone the right to waste someone else's time. Not being interested is one thing. Leaving a man you're dating in limbo with no communication is another. It only takes a minute or two to make a quick call or send an e-mail or text message, even if it's just to make the other guy aware of your current busy schedule and to let him know you want to reconnect when the smoke clears.

Though Jeremy has since reiterated to me how serious he is about forming a full-fledged relationship, I know that until he becomes more reliable and more respectful of others' time, that prospect is unlikely for him.

The Sporadic Elusive Dater

Jeremy could be a card-carrying member of a club I call the Sporadic Elusive Dater, or SPED.

The SPED member gets the ball rolling well with one or more hopeful dating candidates. It looks promising, and he's jazzed! Then all of a sudden things pick up a bit at work, or his dog has the flu, or Mercury goes into retrograde, and *whoosh!* He's SPED away without a trace . . . until his next spurt of dating enthusiasm. His date is left in the dust, without an explanation.

A frequent but flimsy excuse the SPED member uses for his behavior is that he's lost interest and doesn't want to hurt the other guy's feelings. What a crock!

Part of the dating deal is being honest with the other guy. Whenever I ask the students at one of my workshops whether, if a guy decides he's lost interest in them, they'd rather he directly say so to them or not, it's unanimous—they want to know. They don't want to be left in limbo. Would you?

Respect

"R.E.S.P.E.C.T.!" Aretha said it best back in the 1960s, but it still rings true today. There can be no trust without respect and vice versa. If you want to be respected, you must be respectful. How far can a relationship go with an unreliable partner?

Respect means different things to different people. For our purpose, think of respect as treating someone (including yourself) with consideration and reliability. Regardless of whether you've decided he's hot or not, regardless of cultural and social differences, regardless of his income level, and regardless of what other people think, everyone deserves basic respect.

Respect brings out the best in us and re-affirms the importance of us all to each other. When someone claims to have been "disrespected," it can often mean he was treated in an inconsiderate manner. Think of some instances when you felt you were treated disrespectfully. It probably left you feeling angry . . . and downright dissed!

Adding insult to injury is when you're disrespected by that Mr. Handsome-and-Charming you've been dating and may have developed feelings for. Handsome and charming does not equal reliable—sad, but true.

I might be sounding a bit preachy right now, but I'm speaking from the heart. It saddens me that, as a society, we devalue the respect, reliability, and patience needed to treat each other with civility. Having worked with literally thousands of gay men, I truly feel that is a major reason why so many gay men have trouble making authentic connections—too much judging and so little respect.

And They Wonder Why They're Single . . .

Talk about serendipitous . . . I'm right in the middle of writing about a lack of responsibility and respect, and the perfect example drops right in my lap today! Some men sabotage their dating potential before they even start the process.

I am furious! I just got back from my office after quite the frustrating experience with a prospective client. Randy, an executive director in his late twenties, filled out ManMate's online profile about a week ago. I subsequently scheduled an appointment to meet with him last Friday at my office. (I split my time between two offices: one is where I do the matching, communicate with members, and so on, and the other is where I meet new clients, get to know them, and go through their profiles.)

There was a torrential rain last Friday, so right before heading over I called Randy to confirm our appointment. He said he wasn't sure he was going to come, due to the weather, which I understood. (I did wonder, however, if he had planned to give me a quick call to let me know he wasn't coming. I suspected not.) We scheduled another appointment for tonight, which I reconfirmed with him over the phone last night.

Randy was my only appointment, so I made the trip tonight just to meet with him. After waiting for him for fifteen minutes, I called his cell phone. When he picked up, I asked him what was happening with our scheduled appointment for tonight. He said, "Hang on a moment—I'll be right with you" and promptly hung up. He didn't put me on hold—he hung up!

What sort of guy behaves this way? Well, I'll tell you. He's an immature, inconsiderate man who is in no way ready to follow through with dating, much less a relationship.

Thanks for the heads-up, Randy, and for providing me with such a clear example to use to illustrate irresponsible, disrespectful behavior.

Day 5 Weekly "Be Patient, Responsible, and Respectful" Exercises

Self-reflection is really the most authentic way for any of us to see where we stand and how to regard ourselves in the areas of patience, responsibility, and respect. These areas are all subjective, with a large number of variables.

So, for Day 5, take some time to reflect, consider the following, and decide for yourself:

Regarding Patience

- Overall, would you consider yourself a patient person?

- In what area(s) of your life are you the most patient? How has this benefited you?

- In what area(s) of your life are you the least patient? Has this been or could it become detrimental in any way?

- Review the day you had yesterday. Were there times when you were filled with impatience? What was the outcome? Would a conscious attempt at being more patient have helped? If not, what would have?

- In a current or past dating situation, do you or have you found yourself consistently impatient with your date? How could you have improved this situation?

- Do you find yourself frustrated if you don't get instant gratification, whether it's sex, food, praise, or anything else? Have you considered delaying that gratification, making it that much better when the time is right?

- Have trusted friends or family ever suggested that you might be impatient? If so, how did you respond?

Regarding Responsibility

- Overall, would you consider yourself a responsible person?

- In what area(s) of your life are you the most responsible? How has this benefited you?

- In what area(s) of your life are you the least responsible? Has this been or could it become detrimental in any way?

- Review the day you had yesterday. Were there times when you felt overwhelmed with responsibility? How did you handle this? Were there times when you consciously shirked responsibility? What was the result?

- If you shirked responsibility, did anyone else have to take up the slack for you? Or did you have to cover for someone else who is slacking off? How did either of these situations make you feel?

- Do you find yourself angry with others for your problems or challenges? Do you find yourself blaming people for the unhappiness in your life? Take time to be very honest with these questions. It's tough to admit we might have a victim mentality, but it's better to know if it's true.

- Do you take the time to see how you might have made mistakes? Have you figured out what might be learned from your missteps? Have you decided to finally take the wheel in your life to achieve your goals and happiness? If so, you're well on your way out of Victimland—bravo!

Regarding Respect

- Overall, would you consider yourself a respectful person?

- Would you be the type of person you'd like to date? If so, you probably respect yourself and show consideration for other people. If not, do some deep reflection and think how you could show more respect for other people and then ultimately for yourself.

Let me take a moment here to congratulate you on your work so far. By the time you've gotten to this part of the Plan, you are well on your way to reaping the benefits of your efforts. You have spruced up not only on the outside, but, more importantly, within yourself, in areas that will have truly lasting rewards in all aspects of your relationships. I can now help guide you in putting it all together.

DAY 6

Commit

"You're 99.9 percent perfect for me, but I've always seen myself with someone taller. So, this won't work for me . . ."
—Gary GrassIsAlwaysGreener

I know the word "commit" brings up a wide variety of feelings, pro and con, for each of us. For our purposes here, let's take any implied pressure off ourselves.

Commit does not necessarily mean that you have to make the choice to marry someone or move in right away with your current guy. It could mean that eventually, but for now, let's go with the dictionary definition of commitment as "an engagement or pledge to do something." That seems more doable, doesn't it?

Our lives are full of daily commitments. We commit to going to work, attending school, and running errands, not to mention a slew of other pledges we make with our time. But before we are able to make any of these commitments, we have to feel ready and prepared. With the work you've done and will continue to do with this book, you'll eventually feel ready to make a dating or relationship commitment on some level.

- When you meet someone who interests you, you present the authentic you, not some compromised version.

- You have most likely learned to "get real" about yourself and others.

- You are letting go of the past.

- You're ready to move on and balance your life to include a new partner.

- You've become more open and are now extending to that person and are also receptive to him on an ongoing basis.

- You are becoming responsible, as you and your partner are creating another entity—the relationship itself—complete with all its passions and potholes.

- Having learned to be reliable, respectful, and truthful, you can now make the commitment to something much more than a hookup for instant gratification.

Perhaps you are still feeling commitment-phobic, despite the work you've done. Let's take a look at a couple of other guys with commitment issues. Maybe you'll recognize something about yourself in their stories that can help you.

Let's address the above quote by Gary GrassIsAlwaysGreener, shall we? It was actually said to my co-author Dennis, who relayed the painful story to me.

Dennis and Gary

About eight years ago, Dennis met "Gary GrassIsAlwaysGreener" at a cocktail party. They hit it off but did not exchange any contact information. Dennis left the party thinking how attractive Gary was, but never thought they'd connect in the future.

A few days later, Dennis received a call from Gary. He told Dennis that he had asked the host of the party for his number because he thought Dennis was so funny and cute—and how great it was that they were both from the Midwest and about the same size (both about 5'5" or so). He then asked Dennis out to dinner, and they set a date.

Later that day, the host of the party called Dennis and said, "I hope you didn't mind that I gave Gary your phone number. He told me he'd really like to see you again. I think you guys would be good together."

As flattered as Dennis was, he was also quite reluctant to start dating at any level. His last, four-year relationship had ended painfully, so he was feeling extra-cautious. However, Gary pursued him with such fervor that they began spending a great deal of time together.

Dennis told me that at the time it felt like a match made in heaven. They had similar interests and tastes in music and theater, loved each other's company, and had fun sex!

This seemingly heavenly match went on for several months. Looking back on it, Dennis did remark that Gary was incredibly attentive when they were alone. But, with a group of men, Dennis often found it hard to get Gary's attention. (Red flag number one!) But, he let it pass . . .

Gary asked Dennis to drive to Virginia Beach and bring in the new millennium with him and his family. Dennis saw this as a serious relationship overture. After all, bringing in the New Year with someone is already a big deal, but bringing in the year 2000 . . . !!!

Shortly after the New Year, Gary began to avoid Dennis's calls, and when they did get together, it felt awkward. One night, over margaritas at a trendy Mexican restaurant, Dennis brought up his feeling of love and wondered why Gary had become distant. That's when Gary replied, "You're 99.9 percent perfect for me, but I've always seen myself with someone taller. So, this won't work for me."

Obviously, this was devastating for Dennis. But he later realized that Gary was indeed avoiding a commitment of any kind. Dennis came to know that it was easier for Gary to find a fault in him, rather than realize his own fear of not finding the "perfect" person.

I asked Dennis why he didn't notice the warning signs when Gary basically ignored him when other guys were around. Dennis eventually realized that he hadn't wanted to acknowledge the signs because he had been stuck in the past. Gary reminded him a lot of his last boyfriend, and it seemed like, in a sense, he was reliving it all again.

Dennis was then able to put that behind him, and eight months later he met Grant, his real match made in heaven. They're still together today.

Dennis and Gary recently had dinner. Gary apologized for what had happened. He admitted he had ruined the potential for a great relationship because of his fear that commitment of any kind would mean he might lose other possibilities or the control over his feelings. But, he now wanted to make a commitment to a friendship with Dennis.

That's a great start for someone like Gary. His making a commitment for any type of relationship is a big step. However, he's still single and looking for Mr. Perfect. Let's hope "Gary GrassIsAlwaysGreener" gets real regarding commitments before all that grass turns old and brown!

Men who believe "the grass is always greener" are the embodiment of the fear of commitment. When working with these guys, I find that they, indeed, tend to obsess on finding the "perfect" person. They usually want to avoid any inevitable rough patches along the way, so they tend to view any challenge or imperfection that comes up with a prospective partner as grounds to bail and continue the search. Or, on some unspoken level, they realize that they're not ready to commit, so they find something flawed in every potential partner, rather than cop to their own deficiencies.

Some of us avoid commitment by, consciously or not, choosing to pursue potential partners who have issues that as much as guarantee relationship failure. Read on . . .

Lou and the Broken Wing Syndrome

Shortly after I moved to New York City twenty-five years ago, I went to an Upper West Side bar called Cahoots, now long gone. A new acquaintance introduced me to Lou. The minute I met Lou I pretty much knew he would be a close, lifelong friend. I don't know how or why. Sometimes it just happens that way.

During one of our ongoing breakfast powwows through the years, amid countless cups of coffee, Lou and I concluded that the "broken wing syndrome" is one of his challenges.

Lou is youthful, attractive, intelligent, and articulate and one of the funniest men I've ever met. He also pursues men who, in some way, shape, or form, and often by their own admission, are emotionally damaged and in no frame of mind to form a relationship with him, or anyone else, for that matter. It never deterred Lou from persevering and trying to help each one fix his "broken wing" emotional issues.

Lou devoted several years of his life to an on-again-off-again relationship with a much younger man named Jared. Jared was a sensitive and reclusive artist who essentially freeloaded off of Lou for months at a time while sharing very little of himself emotionally and physically in return. Knowing Lou as well as I have for many years, in retrospect I think much of the appeal of being with Jared was that he provided Lou with a challenging emotional project.

Shortly after that relationship ended, Lou became involved with Cary, a workaholic designer who lived over three hours away in a secluded, rural area in upstate New York. Cary ultimately proved to be as remote emotionally as he was geographically. So again Lou was, essentially, provided with an emotional block of ice that he saw as his mission to melt.

During the last several years, Lou has made a major career change from acting to social work, and he's truly excellent at what he does. His days are filled with clients who greatly appreciate his expertise in helping them navigate through their complex emotional issues. Lou now primarily channels his therapeutic abilities into his career, while in his personal life, he seeks out the reciprocating, emotionally available partner he deserves.

Day 6 Weekly "Commit" Exercises

Only you can know whether you're ready to make a step toward commitment in any relationship. Begin by taking stock of how you presently feel overall about dating and potential relationships. This is a very internal exercise and could begin by first reviewing the progress you've made with the past five days' exercises.

Note which issues really jump out at you as you do this review—they are probably your biggest challenges to commitment. Having this knowledge, ask yourself:

- What is really stopping me from committing?

- Is my life out of balance?

- Do I know what I'm looking for?

- Am I being too unrealistic about what I'm looking for?

- Am I looking for physical perfection to the exclusion of all other traits?

- Am I being real about wanting an authentic relationship, or am I really looking for a trophy boyfriend to parade around?

- Do I want a relationship in which I feel best about myself, or do I just want some enjoyable eye candy?

As you begin to answer these questions, or others you may ask yourself, you'll discover what steps to take to overcome your challenges. But, no matter what commitment means to you, pledge to do something! Don't let the fear of commitment rob you of the many joys of dating and loving.

> **"The greener grass on the other side is probably artificial turf."**
> **—Author unknown**

DAY 7

Be Grateful
and Enjoy!

I sincerely hope by the time you've reached Day 7 of the Plan, you'll have gained not only more insight about your true self but also the self-confidence to step out and start dating successfully. You've done a great deal of work, and now it's time to enjoy the fruits of your labor! In this day and age of tremendous stresses and challenges, it can be very easy to forget to enjoy the process. This is the day to invite enjoyment back into your life.

If you think back to when you were a kid, or if you happen to come across some children playing or interacting, take a minute to see how they enjoy just being in the moment—how they delight in simple moment-to-moment discoveries. They haven't learned yet to pre-judge or hide or become inauthentic, and so their enjoyment is spontaneous and real.

As adults, our negative experiences or other life challenges have created so much fear and apprehension that we often don't allow ourselves the freedom to feel joy. By reminding yourself that your next date is not some huge life test and that no one will die or be vilified, you'll be able to actually enjoy the process and not be so affected by the result.

Everyone is more attractive when they're enjoying themselves. You deserve to enjoy your life and relationships! Otherwise, what's the point?

It's also important to enjoy the unexpected. What may at first seem to be problematic or disappointing can often turn out to be something for which you are eternally grateful. An example of this happened to me not too long ago.

ManMate's Home

For eighteen of the twenty-plus years I've owned ManMate, I housed it in a small, quaint office in a stairwell with a beautiful oval window in a landmark building in Manhattan's West 70s. I loved the office and its cozy, informal feel and always thought it helped my new clients feel comfortable and at home. My office neighbors were especially warm and helpful. The surrounding neighborhood also held special memories and meaning for me ever since my first days in New York City. Not to mention the fact that it was a great financial deal! I was very grateful to have that office.

About two years ago, the landlord informed me that the building was being torn down to make way for a new high-rise.

My first feelings were those of disappointment and a sort of emptiness. This had been my unique, little home-away from-home for so many years. Where would I find a new, affordable office with character and a convenient location in crowded, cost-prohibitive Manhattan?

After my initial dismay at the news, I made the choice to think about what could be some positive aspects of losing the space.

With a little consideration, I realized that, cozy and quaint though the office was, ManMate and Dinners for 8 were bursting at the seams in the small space. In addition, whenever I had a meeting with a new client there, it was difficult to converse about the personal details of his life with my associate and assistant present, not to mention the incessant ringing of the phones. My business was expanding, and it was important for me to give it room to grow and continue to thrive. As homey as my office was, it was time to accommodate the professional nature of my clients with a suitable, upscale office.

It eventually occurred to me that what I really wanted was two offices; one for the day-to-day ManMate work and the other as a meeting place for my new clients. My dinner party associate, Greg, mentioned he had previously worked at Rockefeller Center in what is called a "virtual office," where you share the offices with other businesses for however many hours a week you require. This seemed to me to be an ideal arrangement for interviews with new clients and my varying work schedule, so I checked it out.

Sure enough, the staff turned out to be incredibly helpful and friendly. The price included a general receptionist, additional phone line, mailing address, and office equipment—virtually everything I required. It's located closer to my home, and I really enjoy being able to walk or bike there on nice days. Additionally, I found another space nearby for ManMate's day-to-day work, and, even with both offices, I've ended up paying less than the rent on my previous office.

It turned out to be a great lesson for me. By looking for the positive aspects in a seemingly disappointing turn of events, I ended up with so much better than what I had and couldn't be more grateful.

Day 7 Weekly "Be Grateful and Enjoy" Exercises

I truly believe that when we allow ourselves to feel enjoyment and are, in turn, grateful, our lives improve dramatically in all areas. But since my expertise is with dating and relationships, let's find some ways to add enjoyment to your next date.

- Regard the upcoming date as an unexpected bonus that came into your life. Don't see it as another item to check off your daily schedule of requirements. It's supposed to be for your enjoyment and pleasure—it is not a task to be completed!

- Make sure that the place or places you are going on your date are enjoyable to both of you. Why agree to go to a restaurant with food you know you dislike? Some guys will do it just to seem agreeable. But, you'll simply undermine your own enjoyment. Same thing goes for movies, videos, museums, or any other date outings. If you don't feel strongly one way or the other, stay open. Discovery can be incredibly enjoyable.

- Approach every date, first and foremost, as a potential friendship. Don't make your next date an "interview" for your next boyfriend. It's a date, not a casting call. Simply relax and enjoy yourself and the company of your date. As I've said before— don't prejudge—you can't always control the destination, so enjoy the ride!

Gratitude

Gratitude seems to be the New Age mantra du jour. Everyone from Oprah, with her "Gratitude Journal," to Ellen, with her "Life List," is experiencing the transforming power of being in a state of gratitude and being proactive about our life's desires. I couldn't agree more. I've also experienced wonderful results by listing those things for which I'm grateful. It's a way to focus energy and power in a positive direction.

It's relatively easier to be grateful when things go our way or to be appreciative of the people or material things that already make us happy. But, what about being grateful for life's bigger problems or traumatic situations that happen in our lives? That's more challenging and just as, if not more, important.

To start, it's necessary to consider that problems or traumas can be opportunities to learn something and, ultimately, end up in a better, more successful situation. How many times have we all, in retrospect, been grateful that we were dumped by that guy we thought would love us forever, and realized it was the best thing that ever happened? How many of us have gone on to greater success in our work after losing what we thought was the perfect job?

These are just a couple of examples of trauma turning into opportunity. If we are able to understand this when a dating or relationship problem arises, we'll better see the opportunities that await us. I was reminded of how true this is when I met Zach . . .

Zach and Aaron

When he stopped by my office to become a client five winters ago, Zach, an attractive, upbeat thirty-eight-year-old working in real estate, was coming off a very rough year. New to town from Chicago, he had lost his partner of four years in a senseless car accident eight months before. After months of going through, as he put it, "Every feeling I never knew I had," Zach was ready for a new chapter in his life. He had always wanted to try living in New York City and, after recently relocating here, declared, "Now's the time for a new adventure!"

As we began to discuss his recent experiences, I was drawn in by Zach's genuine appreciation of his new day-to-day life here. The combination of a new job, a new home, and being newly single can be unsettling, to say the least. Yet Zach seemed to welcome each fresh experience like an eager student, taking it all in stride, with energy and optimism.

I began to introduce Zach, both one-on-one and through the dinner parties, and his enthusiasm seemed to be infectious. Rarely have I seen so many of my clients enamored of the same guy. What really touched me was hearing a new energy in the voices of some of my most reserved clients, as they related their interest in getting to know him better.

Zach is kind of a regular guy-next-door. He is certainly attractive, but not drop-dead gorgeous, and in decent, but not exceptional, shape physically. What my clients were drawn to was, simply, his "inner spark."

There were a number of promising candidates in our base of men for Zach. Eventually I introduced him to Aaron, a forty-one-year-old architect, and a mutual "spark" was lit. Each year, on their anniversary, I receive a note of gratitude from Zach for the introduction to Aaron. A couple of months ago, they had a civil union ceremony in New Jersey. All my best wishes go out to them.

When you find yourself in what seems to be a crisis, be completely honest as you ask yourself the following:

- How do I feel about this situation?

- What can I learn from this situation?

- What opportunities have now opened up for me?

- What do I, ultimately, have to be grateful for?

> **"Gratitude is not only the greatest of virtues, but the parent of all the others."**
> **—Cicero**

Celebrate!

Congratulations! You have reached the end of Part 1. Before moving on to Part 2, do something fun to celebrate! If you choose to review or rework Part 1, you'll be able to celebrate again when you get to this point. Never miss the chance to celebrate you or your accomplishments!

Now, on to Part 2. It's not just the seven principles that will help you. In this next section, you'll find some must-know approaches to dating, secrets to success, and other such practical and fun advice from your very own "Gay Matchmaker." Enjoy!

PART II

More Practical Advice

from the

Gay Matchmaker

CHAPTER 8

Ask ManMate

Back in the mid-1990s, I wrote an advice column called "Ask Man-Mate" for a now-defunct gay dating/relationship magazine called *ManHunt*. In re-reading those columns years later, I realized that my outlook on many of these dating issues has remained pretty much the same. The following excerpts from my column still essentially encapsulate my point of view. As you read each writer's basic questions, before reading my comments, try answering the questions for yourself.

Regarding HIV disclosure:

Dear ManMate,

Brad and I have had several dates over the past month. Our relationship has been physical but completely safe, and we've gotten to be really close.

Last night I fixed a special dinner for him. I was hoping for a hot, romantic evening. Over coffee and dessert, he suddenly informed me that he is HIV-positive. The news took me completely by surprise. I told him that I thought he should have

*let me know sooner. The conversation got pretty heated up, and I
finally told him I needed some time alone to think.*

*Shouldn't Brad have informed me of his status earlier? Now
that I know, should I consider a possible ongoing relationship
with him? I've grown really attached to him and I'm HIV-
negative.*

—Confused

Dear Confused,

It's true that Brad could have informed you a bit earlier about his
HIV status. But you mentioned you've been safe physically, so no
chance of transmission was involved.

Sharing HIV status can vary based on the individuals involved.
Some guys are immediately upfront and want their prospective partner to know their positive status right away. Other men, like Brad,
may be more private with the information at first. They may choose
to bring it up as they become more comfortable with their partner. As
long as unsafe sex doesn't become an issue, it really comes down to an
individual choice.

Also keep in mind that in dealing with HIV, communication is
a two-way street. You can certainly feel free to broach the subject as
early on as you need to know. You don't need to wait for the other guy
to bring it up.

This brings us to your second question. Only you can answer
whether or not you would consider a relationship with Brad. Through
my work at ManMate, I've found that there are HIV-negative men
who specifically decide that they aren't interested in developing an
ongoing relationship with someone who is HIV-positive. I've also
worked with many HIV-negative guys who are open to the possibility
of having a full-fledged, mixed-status relationship, and I'm aware of
many such relationships that are thriving and completely successful.

I would advise you to trust you own individual instincts. Do a little
honest soul-searching and determine what you feel is most workable
and best for you.

Good luck and please keep me posted.

Regarding Unequal Attraction, follow-through, and respect:

Dear ManMate,

All gay men are jerks! Except for me, and maybe a handful of others. I'm as trustworthy and dependable as a Boy Scout, but I continually meet men who give me the runaround.

My date with Craig last weekend was pretty much typical. After a great time together, he told me he'd call in the next couple of nights. When I didn't hear from him, I left a cute message on his answering machine. It's already the weekend again and no Craig.

Why don't adult men follow through with what they say they're going to do? And if they're not interested, why don't they just say so?

Help! I'm getting paranoid!!!

—Dating Limbo

Dear Limbo,

Calm down. Take a deep breath. These are good questions. We've probably all been on both sides of this issue.

A couple of things may be happening here. Often the feeling of chemistry at an initial encounter is not equal on both sides. Sometimes the guy who is less attracted may avoid being honest, rationalizing that he is sparing the other guy's feelings. This may be how Craig chose to handle your encounter, and it's pretty much a cop-out. It can be frustrating when you just want someone to be straightforward with you, and they don't follow through.

Keep in mind that some men simply don't follow through with potential dating situations in general. They may enjoy the adventurous aspect of meeting someone new, but they aren't willing to put forth the effort to develop it further. Guys who are at this point may be charming on a first date, but they are usually not promising candidates for a more substantial relationship.

Ultimately, with dating—as with most aspects of your life—you tend to get back what you give out. Men who are willing to prioritize meaningful relationships eventually find their way to one another. Keep putting yourself out there. I'll bet there's another Boy Scout just around the corner for you.

Regarding pacing and patience:

Dear ManMate,

I never seem to have a problem meeting attractive guys. I'm good-looking and I'm not shy about approaching someone I'm attracted to at a club or the gym and starting a conversation. In fact, I can usually work things around to a hot sexual encounter later on. But it never seems to go anywhere beyond a one-night stand or a weekend thing.

Friday night was typical. I invited this hot guy I met at the bar over to my house, and we really had a great night together. (Fireworks!) He didn't give me his number, but he got mine and said he'd call me later in the weekend. It's Monday night and no word.

I want a relationship that's going somewhere, and it doesn't seem to be happening. In fact, it's never happened for me. Where am I going wrong?

—*UpperWest Upset*

Dear Upset,

Obviously, you have a talent for making initial connections with guys you're interested in. That's a great quality to have, and it works well for you—to a point. But if you're only using that talent to "work things around to a hot sexual encounter," it's unlikely that it will lead you to the meaningful relationship you say you want. Not to mention the fact that the other guy will be very aware that you view him mainly as a sexual object and will respond accordingly.

Full-fledged, ongoing relationships encompass a lot more than physical attraction and compatibility. The next time you meet someone you sense has dating or possibly relationship potential, rather than wooing him home to bed, set up a one-on-one meeting with him for coffee or a drink. Make it a neutral place—not yours or his—outside a loud, smoky bar or cruisy gym. Since you already know you're physically attracted to him, use the time together to learn other things. What interests do you share? What are some of his basic values? How do you communicate in general?

As gay men, we often tend to over-prioritize physical and sexual attraction. Discovering and appreciating other qualities in a prospective mate goes a long way toward balancing the potential you may have for a more substantial relationship.

Dear ManMate,

Last week I met the first guy in months who seemed like boyfriend potential. Skip is a straightforward, attractive guy with a sense of humor. Right away I felt I could be myself with him.

We spent the whole afternoon together. I did almost all of the talking, and he seemed like a good listener. I pretty much told him everything that has been going on in my life. Since I've been having a rough time getting over a past relationship and working in a boring job I was honest with him about these things right off the bat.

I liked Skip and left a message for him the next day about getting together again. It's been a week and no word. Did I say too much too soon? Honesty is very important to me.

—Tell It Like It Is

Dear Like It Is,

Your desire to be honest is admirable. But wanting to "tell it like it is" doesn't mean you have to tell it all at a first meeting. Skip may have felt overwhelmed with all the information you provided about your life.

First dates are for getting acquainted a bit and discovering potential connections between you. It's important to get things off to a positive start. Interests or points of view that you share are probably better subjects to discuss than broken relationships or unhappy job situations.

Remember that it's a two-way street. It sounds like your meeting with Skip consisted pretty much of a monologue about you and your life. What did you ask or learn about him? A little give-and-take goes a long way toward strengthening your rapport with one another.

Skip may have given you the slip. But next time around, see if you can combine your qualities of being honest and direct with a genuine interest in what's going on with the other guy.

Good luck.

Dear ManMate,

I'm a very attractive, well-built, outgoing guy. My friends tell me I have charisma. I'm also very passionate by nature, and that's a really important aspect of any relationship that I have.

When Juan and I met last month, there was a definite spark. It was clear we were very attracted to each other. We've had a few great dates, and there's been a really strong connection, physically and otherwise. He seemed to appreciate my tendency to be rather intense—at least at first.

I've been very attentive and call him regularly to let him know I'm thinking about him. When something feels right and I like a guy a lot, I figure why not go full speed ahead and flow with the feelings? Lately Juan seems to be pulling back and is acting more distant to me. He told me he thinks it's going too fast.

I'm beginning to feel like I'm doing most of the work to keep the energy and passion going. This is the third potential boyfriend I've met during the past six months with the same situation. I want a full-fledged, committed relationship. Should I give Juan more time, keep searching for a guy who'll match my intensity, or just throw in the towel?

—One Passionate Guy

Dear Passionate Guy,

Don't throw in the towel yet. You're obviously a very attentive guy and focused on following through with a situation that has relationship potential.

You may be moving too quickly in the intensity department. You've only known each other a few weeks. Since you know that connecting with your passionate nature comes naturally to you, see if you can balance it out with other aspects. Being receptive and sensitive to how Juan needs to proceed is very important at this point.

Through years of discussing early dating with guys at ManMate, I've found that pacing is one of the prime challenges that come up. The pacing has to be comfortable for both sides. In other words, it's pretty much a given that you can only move as quickly as the guy who needs to go more slowly, in this case Juan. This involves not only trusting the connection between the two of you, but also trusting him in general.

It's true that there are no guarantees of how any given dating situation will turn out. Perhaps you're being a bit overly attentive with Juan as a way of trying to control how things proceed. Remember that romantic relationships can't ultimately be controlled. See if you can ease off and allow Juan to sort out his feelings. Meanwhile, enjoy his company and don't worry about the outcome. Trust that if it's meant to be, it'll take you there.

Good luck and keep me posted!

Regarding aging:

Dear ManMate,

I'm an attractive, successful guy who's turning forty next year, and I've never had a long-term relationship. I'm always drawn to guys in their early twenties. They seem to have an idealism and boyish enthusiasm that appeal to me. I've had many exciting short-term things with these younger guys, but nothing develops into something more solid. Usually they take it less seriously than I do. Am I limiting myself too much, or is there a chance I could have a meaningful, long-term relationship with someone in this younger age range?

—*Edgy About Turning Forty*

Dear Edgy,

You may well meet a younger guy who fulfills your expectations and is interesting in pursuing a relationship with you. But keep in mind that gay men in their early twenties are often more focused on exploring their sexuality in general than prioritizing a long-term relationship (of course, there are exceptions).

You might want to take a look at what's motivating you right now. Consider why it's so important to you to lock into such a specific age range. Maybe that period in your own life was less than fulfilling. Are you trying to re-experience it with a younger guy to "get it right"? Are you yourself ready for the effort and commitment required of a full-fledged relationship? Pursuing younger men who are less willing to fully commit themselves can be a safe way to avoid a relationship.

Enthusiasm and idealism, the qualities that you mentioned often attract you, can be found in men of any age. As an experiment, try letting go of your age restrictions for a while. In addition to pursuing younger guys, follow through with men closer in age whose energy and outlook appeal to you. Who knows? You might even find a meaningful connection with someone who shares similar life experiences and values as well as a comparable birth date.

Regarding obsession, getting real, and responsibility:

Dear ManMate,

Several weeks ago I met this really hunky guy. Lance is gorgeous, with a perfect body. My ideal fantasy! (I'm reasonably good-looking, if not Adonis material.)

We only went out once. It seemed to go OK, although I'm not sure how interested he was. When I've called him since, he's always been nice but never suggests getting together again. I'm kind of shy, so I guess I want him to initiate another date.

My problem is that since I've met him, I don't seem to have much interest in seeing other guys. I compare them, and no one measures up to Lance physically. I find myself thinking about him all the time. It's like this incredible fantasy! But waiting for the phone to ring is getting boring, especially since he's never actually called me.

What can I do? What can I say? I'm . . .

—Obsessed

Dear Obsessed,

Yep. That's the word for it.

You certainly have patience, but you also may be a bit reluctant to get to whatever the truth is. It seems easier for you to obsess on Lance as a fantasy figure than to proceed to any real possibility.

You haven't mentioned anything else you know or like about him. Is physical attraction your only criterion? If so, you might want to think about whether it's worth it to devote so much energy to an image obsession.

Saying that you're too shy to ask him for another date is a bit of a cop-out. If you've been assertive enough to call him a few times, asking him out now should be a snap.

So snap out of this funk! Rather than waiting for Lance to get off his hunky butt and call you, take the plunge. Ask him out. Clearly and directly.

Since this is so important to you, be prepared to be flexible with your schedule when you call him. That way, if he is interested, you can make a definite date and move forward.

Also, be prepared for a rejection. But remember that a specific "no" from him could also help you let go of being in limbo over a fantasy. You could then proceed to more concrete possibilities. Sometimes a flesh-and-blood, slightly imperfect guy with an ability to meet you halfway can be just the ticket.

Regarding honesty:

Dear ManMate,

Last night I had my first date with Hank. He's a very friendly and attentive guy, but I didn't feel any initial spark with him and wasn't interested in a second date. As we were saying goodnight, Hank asked me if I'd like to spend Gay Pride Day together. Without thinking, I said "Sure," even though I'd rather spend the day with a couple of close friends.

This is turning into a pattern for me. I can't seem to communicate to guys when I'm not interested. Then I usually stop returning their phone calls, so that I don't have to reject them directly.

Why do I have trouble turning a guy down? And what could I have said when Hank asked me out again?

—I Can't Say No

Dear Can't Say No,

You may be overly concerned you'd be hurting the other guy's feelings by saying "No." Or maybe you want to avoid what you're afraid would be an uncomfortable confrontation. (I've even spoken to men who feel they're doing the other guy a favor by accepting a date they don't want, when in reality they're just postponing rejecting him.) You also may enjoy the feeling of being pursued for a while. But not returning phone calls and leaving the other guy up in the air is irresponsible, unkind, and simply dishonest.

First meetings don't always—or even usually—indicate future dating or relationship potential. And most men simply want honesty when it comes to knowing whether or not their attraction is returned after a first date. The direct, tactful approach usually works best. In your encounter with Hank, you could have mentioned that you enjoyed meeting him, but that you don't see it as an ongoing dating or romantic situation. This way you've been straightforward with him, Hank won't have further expectations, and both of you are free to direct your energies elsewhere.

If you enjoyed spending time with him, you could also suggest getting together as friends. Hank may or may not take you up on it, but at least you've been upfront and given him a choice.

There's still time to communicate your thoughts with him before Pride Day. You might mention that you'd like to include your friends. That way you could all march together in solidarity.

Happy Gay Pride!

Regarding extending and getting real:

Dear ManMate,

My life is just about perfect. Unfortunately, I can't seem to find the perfect man to share it with.

I'm an attractive, well-built, take-charge kind of guy. My life is busy, and I don't really have the time to devote to dating men who don't have potential. So I've gotten adept at determining whether or not a guy is "boyfriend material" during a first date.

I find that most men just don't measure up to my standards. There always seems to be something about them that I sense won't fit into the scheme of my life, or they don't fit the requirements of my mental checklist. So rather than pursue someone who falls short of what I want, I cross him off my list.

I'm used to being in control with everything else in my life. But I've never had a significant relationship. How can I make it happen?

—Looking for Mr. Right

Dear Looking,

Actually, it's difficult to "make it happen" at the start of any potential relationship. It's a gradual, step-by-step process as you get to know someone, and there's no way of knowing what the outcome is going to be. This may be unsettling for someone who is used to being in control as you are.

Beginning a new relationship involves reaching out to someone else, not simply judging him and analyzing his pros and cons—this is a human being, not a new home entertainment system! As you approach new dating situations, try shifting gears. Rather than evaluating his actions, make a real connection with him. Use your take-charge abilities to steer the conversation toward interests or outlooks you may have in common. In short, concentrate on what you yourself are bringing to the encounter, rather than what you hope to get.

Also keep in mind that no guy, including yourself, is going to be the perfect man you mentioned you're looking for. So, quit putting that pressure on him and on yourself. Put aside your "mental checklist" . . . at least in the beginning. No one is going to meet all your requirements. Part of getting to know someone is learning to accept his quirks along with his strong points.

I know we've all heard this before, but building a relationship takes time and effort. With your busy schedule and loads of available men, it's tempting to discard anyone who isn't "Mr. Right" right away. But if a long-term relationship is really your intention, you need to give yourself time to explore all the possibilities.

Good luck.

Regarding first dates:

Dear ManMate,

I admit it. I'm a klutz when it comes to first dates. If there's a way to screw it up, you can bet I'll find it. How about some help with pinpointing the biggest problems regarding first meetings? I want to avoid the pitfalls and get this year off to a good start.

—SoHo Screwup

Dear SS,

You got it. Based on years of discussing first dates with the guys at ManMate, I present my Top 10 list of the most common issues that come up.

Top 10 Dating Tips

1. *Choice of place to meet.* Very important. Make it a quiet, neutral place outside your home or apartment and away from noisy gay bars. You want to be able to communicate easily.

2. *Focus on the other guy.* Since this is a new opportunity to connect, avoid distractions. Relate directly to him and listen to what he has to say. This is especially helpful if you tend to be nervous or quiet at first.

3. *Balance the conversation.* Don't monopolize it with a rambling verbal resume about yourself or accomplishments. This is a first date, not a job interview. Give and take.

4. *Stay in the present.* Avoid talking about ex-boyfriends or any horror stories from the past. Believe me, he doesn't want to hear about it on your first meeting. Concentrate on interests or points of view you have in common. Deal with now, not then.

5. *Positive energy.* Let's face it. First impressions are important. If you're exuding negative energy or a rigid demeanor, what man is going to be interested? Lighten up.

6. *Getting sexual right away.* Doesn't usually work out. Allow yourself time to balance physical attraction with other important elements like basic communication and similar outlooks and interests. Give it a chance to be more than a sexual encounter.

7. *Pacing.* You can't take a relationship faster than the pace at which *both* guys are comfortable. In other words, if you tend to be more intense or serious than the other guy, ease up. Allow him time to discover how he feels and wants to proceed. Let go of needing to control the outcome.

8. *Unequal attraction.* This means tuning into vibes from the other guy. Be honest with yourself. Often the level of attraction is not equal. If you sense your attraction to him is not really reciprocated, don't try to force the issue. Let it go and direct your energy toward a more promising candidate. If you're the one who's less interested, let the other guy know as quickly and tactfully as possible. Don't leave him in limbo.

9. *Follow-through and respect.* Unreturned phone calls and lack of follow-through are a real drag. We've probably all been on both sides of this issue. It's really simple. Have enough respect for each other to follow through and communicate where things stand. That way you can both move forward.

10. *Special quality.* You've got it. Acknowledge it to yourself and let it come through on all your future first and subsequent dates.

CHAPTER 9

More Dating Tips
from the
Gay Matchmaker
(for First Dates, Blind Dates, and All Dates, for That Matter)

When I re-read the Top 10 list I wrote back in the 1990s, I realized that the ten points made are still completely relevant today. It just shows us how dating issues are universal and timeless.

However, I wanted to expand on this list for the twenty-first century! The world has gotten so much busier and seems so much smaller due to all the technology that's come our way. There are many new ways to meet or contact greater numbers of men—cell phones, digital camera phones, blackberries, text messaging, e-mail, chat rooms, live web cams, and so on. But, with all this "help," newer issues have arisen.

So . . .

More Hot Dating Tips

- Be careful not to date too many men at a time. Technology has made it so much easier to contact more guys, but that doesn't mean you have to meet them all! I'd suggest choosing three to four guys at the most. If you meet too many guys too quickly, you run the risk of dating "burnout" and perhaps missing that special someone.

- Keep your first contact with a potential date short and sweet. Refrain from making too many calls or e-mails or text messages or whatever before your actual first date. Too much contact before you meet can bring about unrealistic or inaccurate assumptions. "Googling" the guy before your first date is an option I'd avoid!

- On a first date, it's usually best for both guys to meet at the designated place. That way, either is free to leave when he feels it's time to go, and there's no dependence on each other for getting home. By the second date, it is a nice overture for one guy to offer to pick up the other. If you both are drivers, you may want to take turns driving on future dates.

- This one's not new but bears repeating: If you're driving, identify the designated driver, so no one drives under the influence.

- Turn off your cell phone during a first date and put it away! You are there to get to know a new guy, not to catch up on correspondence. This goes for all your other toys, too! Answering the phone during a first date won't impress the guy. He won't think, "Wow, he's so popular and important!" He'll just think you're a jerk.

- If you plan to meet at a restaurant, make sure it's a place that's suitable for you both. More and more people are diet- and health-conscious and have more stringent food requirements.

- Because there are so many ways to communicate verbally these days, it is important to also remember to pay attention to body language.

   When you first approach your date, walk with your head up and shoulders back. It gives you a look of confidence and openness.

   When you greet your date, do so with a genuine smile, not a forced, cheesy one. By all means, look him in the eye as you grasp his hand. Make your handshake firm and warm, but not so aggressive as to jolt him or put him off.

   Stay confident and pleasant if you sit down. Slouching with your arms crossed can make you look defensive or even bored. Sit up and keep your hands and arms relaxed.

   If you remain standing, stand straight and still. Shuffling from leg to leg makes you seem unnerved. Keeping your feet and legs slightly apart will maintain a look of confidence.

   Refrain from playing with your hair or face or covering your mouth while you chat. It can make you look unsure of yourself. It can also give the impression that you might not be totally upfront and honest.

   Don't let nervousness cause you to do anything unsightly, such as put your finger in your ear, pick at your nose, or bite your nails. Breathe and maintain friendly eye contact if you start to feel fidgety.

   Remember to respect personal space—even on a crowded city street or restaurant. As a general rule, keep at least 3 feet between you to start out. Later on, leaning in or touching your date gently on the arm or shoulder is fine, if it feels natural and he's giving the right signs. If he keeps moving away from you, you're either too close, you need to be more hygiene-conscious, or he's simply not interested. Stay tuned in—you'll figure it out.

Most importantly, stay relaxed and be yourself. If you do this, many of these tips will take care of themselves, and you won't look self-conscious. Keep in mind, he's nervous too! Acknowledging your nervousness could be very endearing and a great way to break the ice.

CHAPTER 10

Compatibility

We've spent a good deal of time so far helping you to present your best authentic self. Now, how can you tell if you're compatible with that hot guy you've had your eye on?

Compatibility and chemistry are subjective issues. There is no definitive method to determine whether sparks might fly between you and a potential date. There are many ways to determine possible levels of compatibility, but when it comes right down to it, it's really a matter of timing and everything else falling into place.

Let's look at some places to start when determining potential compatibility.

Partner Qualities

When I'm interviewing a new client, I always ask him, "What important compatible qualities do you look for in a partner?" Here's a list you might want to consider as you answer the question for yourself:

- Comfortable with himself and self-sufficient

- Can easily express emotions and feelings

- Does not consider himself a victim, but faces problems

- Not only listens, but hears

- Can give as well as receive

- Comfortable with his sexuality and sexual preferences

- Compatible with me sexually

- Compatible with me intellectually

- Similar life experience

There may be other qualities, but that list will get you motivated to take stock of what's important to you.

Is It in the Stars?

Where does astrology fit, if at all, in the process of finding Mr. Right? I think we'd all agree that "What's your sign?" is a baaaaad first question to ask a promising candidate!

Let's be honest. Many of us have, at times, through our dating travels and travails, turned to the zodiac for a little guidance. Ultimately, it seems to me, the real question is: If we choose to use astrology, how do we use it to our advantage to illuminate potential compatibility, without erroneously nixing possible mates with real potential?

Let me say first off that astrology is a casual avocation of mine. I've had my own horoscope done a few times, taken a couple classes, and, on occasion, "read" some friends' astrological charts for fun. I have often found the information illuminating, to an extent.

Occasionally, certain ManMate clients will ask me to tell them an introduction's Sun sign. I have mixed feelings about giving it out. Although I do believe that there is an element of truth in how various Sun signs relate to one another, I also know that it is *all* the aspects of a guy's chart combined that indicate the most authentic composite of his qualities, character challenges, and potentials. It concerns me when clients have rigid, preconceived notions about certain signs, because other aspects in a man's entire horoscope can flavor, influence, and even overrule the essence of his particular sign.

So, if you're not a professional astrologer, but you're a bit fascinated by what certain Sun sign compatibility indicates, I suggest first getting a sense of the basic qualities of each of the twelve zodiac signs. For some insight and more than a few laughs, I recommend gay astrologer Jill Dearman's book, *Queer Astrology for Men*. It gives you the basics, it's perceptive, it's full of kink, and it's a hoot!

After you've boned up on whatever you choose to read about astrology, think of it as a tool you can pull out whenever you want (now that sounds suggestive!). Then, when you eventually find out a GuyWithPotential's sign, you can use it as a way to empathize with, rather than simply judge, the challenges and potentials indicated for his particular sign. Then, cut him a break—we all have our challenges!

Again, remember, his astrological sign only indicates part of his essence, at most. As I see it, getting real with what your gut feelings tell you about him ultimately trumps what his Sun sign description suggests. Did I mention to enjoy the process? We're not talking about brain surgery here!

Some Lighthearted Fun

Any relationship needs to start with a good friendship. Knowing this to be true, my dinner party associate, Greg, and I put together a fun little personality test to determine compatibility with your man of choice.

These questions are a brief, lighthearted take on some of the questions I use to match clients during face-to-face interviews with new members of ManMate and ManMate Dinners for 8. This is just for fun, but it might actually help clue you in as to whether or not the guy you're dating may be the guy you're with for years to come. If you're single, these questions provide food for thought the next time love comes a-callin'.

Go Away with Me or Get Away from Me!

1. Last summer, you and your ideal boyfriend had a share in a country house with a great group of guys. As this summer approaches, you . . .
   a. get on the phone and make sure that you and your man are included again this year.
   b. expect your ideal boyfriend will take care of it.

   Your ideal boyfriend . . .
   a. took care of this weeks ago.
   b. was happy to hear that you arranged everything.

2. You and your ideal boyfriend are planning a dinner party. Your first thought is . . .
   a. a schedule of tasks that include grocery shopping and cleaning the house.
   b. an interesting new recipe for the perfect appetizer to go with Chilean sea bass.

   Your ideal boyfriend's first thought is . . .
   a. "How do we fit eight guests around a table that's designed to seat four?"
   b. "We've got to highlight the tablecloth to contrast with the arugula in the salad course."

3. The two of you just saw *Beaches* for the sixth time. You . . .
   a. try to calculate the exact amount of collagen that Barbara Hershey received before filming.
   b. cry every time that bitch Hillary dies.

   Your ideal boyfriend . . .
   a. can't understand why we have to watch this sappy movie again.
   b. is misty-eyed and needs a hug.

4. You and your man are planning to go on a fabulous two-week vacation. Your idea of a fabulous vacation is . . .

a. a meticulously scheduled tour of Europe.

b. a cycling trip through Europe wherever your mood takes you.

Your ideal boyfriend . . .

a. immediately Googled "Down Under without Surprises."

b. immediately Googled "Bungee Jumping through Australia."

Scoring: After completing the quiz, fill in the blanks with the letter that matches your answer for that question:

Your answers:					Your ideal boyfriend's answers			
—	—	—	—		—	—	—	—
1	2	3	4		1	2	3	4

Personality Types and Their Characteristics

AAAA "Perfectionist" Peter: Will rearrange your closets (and will want them to stay that way). Always willing to learn. Works hard, plays hard.

BAAA "Efficient" Eric: Always prepared. Responsible and a strong shoulder. Can plan a trip and pack for it perfectly.

ABAA "Leader" Leon: This guy means business. Probably has an upper management position with a Fortune 500 company. Really knows what terms like "mentoring" and "empowering" mean. Might need a helping hand every once in a while to come down from his ivory tower.

AABA "Diplomatic" Darius: A combination of church lady and candy striper. Will listen to your problems and come up with perfect solutions. Keeps things light, pleasant, and fresh smelling.

AAAB   "Head Cheerleader" Hector: In charge and orderly. A deal maker. Enjoys the rewards of his labor. Always gives advice. A charmer.

BBAA   "Self-Control" Sal: Achievement and self-control in spades. Looks kind of lost at parties.

BABA   "Nice Guy" Neil: Heads up committees at the Center. Still uses his grandmother's recipe for tapioca. Will never forget your birthday. Wonders why "we can't all just get along."

BAAB   "Analyzing" Anton: Knows the difference between a socket wrench and a pair of pliers. Will take apart your espresso maker to see how it works. Has absolutely no idea how to react to any of your emotions.

ABBA   "Guiding" Gabriel: Talks on the phone a lot. Has lots of friends. Knows how to make long-term relationships work. Probably has a working knowledge of astrology. Always a little bit ahead or lagging just behind everyone else.

ABAB   "Innovative" Ivan: This alpha male will lead you exactly where you need to go, whether you know it or not. Saves his pennies. Laughs with you—not at you.

AABB   "Showtime" Sean: Great clothes and knows how to wear them. A natural performer and the center of attention. Will ask for your phone number in an elevator.

BBBA "Peer Counselor" Percival: Has read almost every self-help book ever written. Probably knows what his totem animal is. Possibly clairvoyant. Can facilitate a workshop.

BBAB "Designer" Desmond: Might not know which way is up, but knows what glamour is, baby!

BABB "Put It Together" Pierre: Turns lemons into margaritas. Keeps an eye on (your) bottom line. Might not know how truly fabulous he is.

ABBB "Explorer" Eddie: The guy in charge of the time-share. Knows what's going on when no one else does. Actively looking for Mr. Right. Knows what he wants and knows how to get it.

BBBB "Go with the Flow" Guido: Knows the words to Grateful Dead songs. Marches and carries a sign during Gay Pride. Definitely not the "tidy" type because "tidy" is not as important as world hunger.

CHAPTER 11

Where *the* Boys Are

"Where are all the men?" It's a question we've probably all asked at one time or another. Of course, it's a loaded question. It depends on who's asking it and what they're looking for. But, just for fun, I took the question literally and did some research to find out just where the gay men are. Here's what I found:

- The U.S. Bureau of the Census estimates that there are over 113,000,000 adult men in the United States and that approximately 10 percent are gay. That means that there are about 11,300,000 gay men in the United States! Of these men, about 70 percent claim to be single and want a relationship! That's over 7 million available men out there! With these numbers, how can anyone say, "There's no one out there for me"?

- So, where do these 7 or so million men live? Believe it or not, they live all across the United States—according to the census takers. Of course, there are many areas where gay men tend to be more closeted, due to all sorts of reasons. But, they're out there! Even more reason to be ready when the opportunity to date presents itself.

- ePodunk.com is a website I found that actually has a "gay male index" for cities and towns in the United States. It's a great way to find out "where the boys are" and to what degree. The gay index is a comparative score, based on the percentage of gay men reporting in the 2000 U.S. Census. A score of 100 is the national norm (approximately 10 percent of the total male population). A number above 100 indicates that the local proportion of gay men is higher than the national average. For example, 140 would mean that the proportion was 40 percent higher than the national norm, or 14 percent. A score of 60 would be 40 percent lower, or 6 percent, and so on. Remember, these numbers are only approximations based on research, not the gospel. But, they're fun. Also, these numbers are not the total number of gay men in an area, but the proportion of gay men to the total male population. Here are the gay male index scores (from higher to lower) for some U.S. metropolitan areas, gay destinations or just an area near you (Source: www.epodunk.com):

Above the National Average of 100, or 10.0%

- San Francisco, CA   696, or 69.6% (The highest—no surprise there!)

- Ft. Lauderdale, FL   589, or 58.9%

- Atlanta, GA   419, or 41.9%

- Washington, DC   380, or 38.0% (God Bless America!)

- Seattle, WA   371, or 37.1%

- Minneapolis, MN   309, or 30.9% (My hometown!)

- Boston, MA   285, or 28.5%

- Dallas, TX   254, or 25.4% (They say everything's bigger in Texas!)

- Denver, CO   249, or 24.9%
- San Diego, CA   226, or 22.6%
- Sarasota, FL   223, or 22.3% (My other home!)
- Salt Lake City, UT 216, or 21.6%
- Portland, OR   209, or 20.9%
- Los Angeles, CA   204, or 20.4% (Hurray for Hollywood!)
- New Orleans, LA   199, or 19.9%
- Tampa, FL   199, or 19.9%
- Miami, FL   190, or 19.0%
- Chicago, IL   186, or 18.6%
- Phoenix, AZ   178, or 17.8%
- St. Louis, MO   178, or 17.8%
- New York, NY   174, or 17.4% (I thought NYC would be higher up the list, too!)
- Austin, TX   172, or 17.2%
- Houston, TX   169, or 16.9%
- Kansas City, MO   162, or 16.2%
- Richmond, VA   153, or 15.3%
- Baltimore, MD   144, or 14.4%
- Birmingham, AL   144, or 14.4%
- Hartford, CT   139, or 13.9%
- Las Vegas, NV   138, or 13.8%
- Philadelphia, PA   136, or 13.6%
- Charlotte, NC   132, or 13.2%

- Indianapolis, IN   131, or 13.1%
- Charleston, SC   122, or 12.2%
- Tucson, AZ   118, or 11.8%
- Pittsburgh, PA   116, or 11.6%
- Milwaukee, WI   115, or 11.5%
- Cincinnati, OH   115, or 11.5% (And it's nicknamed "The Queen City"!)
- Honolulu, HI   115, or 11.5%
- Des Moines, IA   114, or 11.4%
- Oklahoma City, OK 105, or 10.5%

And Below the National Average of 100, or 10.0%

- Detroit, MI   85, or 8.5%
- Wichita, KS   82, or 8.2%
- Anchorage, AK   86, or 8.6%
- Dover, DE   82, or 8.2%
- Lincoln, NE   61, or 6.1%
- Pocatello, ID   60, or 6.0%
- Fargo, ND   57, or 5.7%
- Cheyenne, WY   49, or 4.9%

Please don't be concerned if I didn't mention your town. If you're still curious, just go to www.epodunk.com to find out more.

CHAPTER 12

Fear versus Love

Fear!

On June 15, 2006, I had a personal breakthrough regarding some of my own issues and fears in writing this book. To release my inner thoughts, I often use an invaluable tool called "morning pages," which I came across in an incredible book I highly recommend called *The Artist's Way,* by Julia Cameron. Shortly after I get up in the morning, I write approximately three longhand, stream-of-consciousness pages. A lot of people prefer to use the exercise as a form of "brain drain," simply putting down whatever comes to mind. For me, writing the morning pages is an effective way of tapping into my gut feelings while affirming what I know, at my core, to be true. Normally I wouldn't share private morning pages, but here they are anyway:

Morning pages, 6/15/2006

I want to be up front—admit that my own fears have prevented me from writing this book sooner. I need to be honest and aware of these fears to be an example—an illustration—of working through fears to get to the only real and simple truth—love.

So, what fears come up? Many, as fear itself creates other fears that have stolen my fire before and convinced me I'm not able to find happiness—realize my dreams.

Most nagging fear—all that I have to say has already been said. I do think that's true—in a sense. The difference is I have my own, unique voice. Going through shelves in a bookstore, there are lots of books on the same subject. But each writer has his or her own unique understanding. I can chuck this fear.

No one has my years of experience—a wealth of stories and examples dealing with gay men looking for relationships. My successes—love of my work conquers my fear of writing. Writing's how I reach an audience in the simplest, most direct way. It's a complicated, chaotic time—people want things direct, simple—to the point.

I shoot from the hip. I'm a gay matchmaker. I'm not a psychologist, but I do "mini-counseling" with clients. I listen to their evolving situations week-to-week, month-to-month. I want to continue to guide them through their challenges, in the most direct, practical ways.

Another fear—how to deal with naysayers—those who dismiss my ideas as too simplistic. I know my principles appear simple, but the process to success takes commitment—work. I don't think relationships aren't complicated. They are. But problems that come up moment to moment come from some basic type of fear—fear of rejection, fear of abandonment, fear of parental disapproval, fear of being exposed, fear of getting old, fear of no longer being attractive, etc., etc. It's a matter of working through whatever the fear is, one situation at a time. It's about courage, bravery—facing the real truth. I feel it's working in my life. I have faith and belief in what I'm doing.

My point of view may not ring true to everyone. We're all at different points in our growth. Some people may feel they're more evolved socially, intellectually—when they create a whirl of complication and drama around themselves. That's simply another point of view.

The hardest fear I've had to deal with is that I won't be perfect, and that this book won't be perfectly rendered. I've always dealt with feeling like I had to present things in a perfect way. Maybe from my upbringing—an atmosphere of everything being in its place—having the veneer of harmony, balance, and order.

The truth is that I won't be perfect. There's nowhere to go from perfection. I can't really identify with it anyway. I can identify with human foibles. We're all flawed. I'm flawed, which I find to be a great relief. I've gotten past trying to be, gotten to the point of not even wanting to be, perfect. I just continue to work through the challenges in my life.

Where Is the Love?

I believe that in any dating or relationship situation, we can either be motivated by some form of fear or by some form of love. I am reminded of this as I reread what I wrote about my own fears.

In the workshops I teach from time to time, I emphasize the concept of fear versus love. Below I've included some actual quotes from some of my students. They can really put it right out there! Their responses were to my question, "What dating issues or fears are you currently facing, and how do you feel about them?"

You'll probably identify with one or more of these responses. Now, with the work you've done in this book, you'll be better equipped to move through these and other fears or challenges that come along in your own life and replace them with the appropriate positive actions, beliefs, attitudes, values, or points of view, which I refer to as "love." As you read these quotes, think about how you yourself might now respond if that particular challenge came into your dating life or relationship, or what advice you might give to a friend in that situation.

> "I haven't dated for four years because of my fear. Is there a man out there who has any sensitivity? It just brings up so much sadness, because I continually lose myself in a man and get so negative about myself. Yet I really want to be in a relationship."
>
> **—Ross**

"He thought we were not at the same place. He thought I looked at the world with wide-eyed wonder, and I thought he looked at it with negativity. I spent lots of dollars on therapy and a lot of training to get my attitude, but still it hurts."
—Stan

"My dates say things like, 'Wow, you're fabulous! You're so interesting! I'll call you!' and then I never hear from them again."
—Lanford

"I'm not into sex on the first date, so often I don't hear back from men I date."
—Yves

"I have just never thought of myself as attractive. I don't know if anyone would really want to be with me. Also, I'm not sure whether I should be with a man or a woman."
—Rich

"I have always been the aggressor and get into relationships with 'bad boys' or married men. This used to be exciting to me, but I want to be with someone who's right for me. It's just that the sex with the 'bad ones' is so great!"
—Cameron

"I'm always the one who does the listening and that seems to work for the people I date since they do all the talking, especially about themselves. I guess I'm just not that exciting. Plus, I'm really very shy."
—Tomas

"Yes, you can connect with guys on the Internet. Boy, have I connected! But, no real connection and most of the guys you meet lie about themselves and then try to cover up for it when you actually meet them—like that makes it OK, and you'll still want to have sex with them!"

—Jeff

"Career versus relationship thing—you can't have it all."

—Jake

"There's been a lot of unhappiness in my relationships, but I stay in them anyway. It's the upbringing I had, I guess—you make the marriage work regardless of what the reality is."

—Brent

"Where am I going to meet someone who's not a potential "ho," who doesn't want just a one-night stand? I want someone who represents himself as real."

—Manuel

"They're going to leave me anyway, so what's the use?"

—Hal

"It just seems too overwhelming to bring another person into my life."

—Phillip

"Do I want to develop something with someone when I don't feel developed myself?"

—Justin

"I don't trust the other person."
                    —Carlos

"A lot of people like me, but no one wants to date
   me."
                    —Pedro

"I give too much."
                    —Scott

"I don't deserve to have the best qualities in another person or to look for high standards."
                    —Ryan

"I'm afraid if I'm honest and stand up for myself,
   I'll be left."
                    —Kirk

"At my age, I feel old with nothing to show for
   it. I don't have the right amount of money, the
   right clothes, the right body type. I'm embar-
   rassed because all those things are so important
   today. Why would a man want me when he can
   go after a younger guy who has more of these
   things? I was always told when a man gets past
   forty, he becomes invisible to other guys. I have
   such shame about that."
                    —Colin

"I never seem suitable enough for a long-term
   relationship. It always seems to fall apart after
   three or four months."
                    —Ben

"I've gotten to the point where I'm afraid to meet anyone because of how they perceive me. After so many rejections, I just don't want to."
—Raj

"I don't want to give up my sense of freedom."
—Roy

"I'm too particular. I want this, this, and that."
—Hunter

"Fear less, hope more;
Whine less, breathe more;
Talk less, say more;
Hate less, love more;
And all good things are yours."
—Swedish proverb

CHAPTER 13

My Story, *in* Brief

One reason I feel especially qualified to write this book is that I have experienced and worked through so many of the challenges I've addressed in it. In fact, you're about to read about some of them firsthand! Unlike the large number of dating/relationship authors I've come across through the years who seemed to be perpetually single, I'm currently in a successful, long-term relationship. But the road there was far from easy . . .

I grew up in wholesome, progressive Minneapolis, Minnesota. I guess from a very young age, I tried to be the good and perfect little boy. I knew pretty early on that I was attracted to other boys and didn't see them having similar feelings. Since I thought my feelings were wrong, I wanted to make sure that I did just about everything else in my life right, or perfectly. Sound familiar to anyone?

My dad has always been a real jock. For several years during my adolescence, he coached my baseball and basketball teams and taught me other sports as well. I'll always be grateful to him for that. At the same time, I had an ongoing fear that he would hear the occasional taunts from other boys of me being a sissy. I remember trying to keep a very low profile on the sports field.

Feeling pretty much like a loner, I tended to gravitate to things I could excel in by myself. I became a proficient piano player and accompanied the school choir and musicals. I got on the teen board of a department store, sold young men's clothes at their Varsity Shop, and modeled on the weekends. I jogged almost everywhere by myself, with no gay boy kindred spirit in sight.

I continued to hide my sexuality through my undergrad years. At the college I attended in the middle of Iowa, I joined a fraternity and acquired a girlfriend. Cat became a soul mate . . . in every way but sexually. My straight façade remained intact.

After graduating, to suppress my increasingly beckoning sexual urges, I became BobbyBusyBusy. I sang, acted, modeled, and taught my way around the Twin Cities for the next couple of years. Finally, during the time I was performing in a supper club show group called Sunshine (that's right, Sunshine. It was the swinging seventies, after all!), my gay roommate, a fellow Sunshine performer, helped me ease out of the closet . . . Thanks, Ron!

I moved to New York City in the early 1980s with dreams of theatrical success. Having gotten my MFA in acting from the University of Minnesota, I was ready to take NYC by storm! For three years I acted and sang, joined the three actors' unions, and did a fair amount of film and soap work, commercials, and theater. My career was off to a pretty good start.

In 1985, my friend John mentioned that he wanted me to join him in starting up a dating service for gay men. We were both single, and the venues for meeting compatible, relationship-oriented guys in NYC at that time were limited. So, what the heck! We went ahead and created ManMate.

After a year, John moved on from ManMate but encouraged me to take it over solo. Run a gay dating service by myself while pursuing an acting career? Sure—why not? As I juggled all aspects of a dating business with an acting career and all that entails, my life became lopsided for a few years, essentially all about work. Suffice it to say, the other areas of my life suffered. I soon gave up live theater acting for the time being, while I ran ManMate at night and kept pursuing my on-camera work.

The combination of being a gay matchmaker and an actor who is up for straight romantic roles on daytime soaps and young daddy roles in TV commercials was unsettling for me, and I started to get a bit paranoid. Although it's still tricky for gay actors to play on-camera leading man roles today, back in the 1980s, it was even more so. What was my solution? I changed my name as the owner of ManMate to Grant Foster and used my real name, Grant Wheaton, otherwise.

Grant Foster. Like the sunglasses, only reversed. Cute, huh? Not really. Since entries in the Manhattan phone book are listed last name first, for years I intercepted hundreds of calls intended for the Foster Grant eyewear company! Talk about not getting real. For the ten years I went by the name Grant Foster at ManMate, I never felt right about the dishonesty of it.

I actually maintained my dual-career balancing act until the end of the 1990s. Thank God for my incredible string of actor/singer/ dancer/model assistants through those years! I want to acknowledge as many of them as I can remember at the end of this book. They were invaluable to me, each in his own way. I truly loved their energy . . . and we could talk shop between all the ManMate phone calls.

I gradually realized that I was becoming increasingly more fulfilled with my work at ManMate—the work with clients, the matchmaking, the workshops, the coaching—than with my work as an actor. I guess I'm an entrepreneur at heart. But more than that, I found I was more interested in the extending to others necessary for matchmaking than the self-involvement that's essential for every actor. Ironically, the scene of my last on-camera acting role was a New Millennium's Eve party on the soap *As the World Turns*.

In the late 1980s, I met the man who would be my partner for the next nine years. Steve and I were great companions who got along well, shared a lot of interests, and took some fabulous trips together. As the years went by, there was clearly something missing in our relationship. We really didn't open up and extend to each other emotionally. It should have been apparent to me, especially when, about five years into it, I instigated an important conversation about our relationship, and after a brief, heated discussion, he replied, "Do we really need to talk about this for more than five minutes?" I let it go.

We also maintained separate apartments and spent most evenings at his place but never actually moved in together. I think that made it easier to avoid a deepening commitment to one another. By the time we sought out a couple's counselor, too much water had gone under the bridge, as they say. I moved the few possessions I had out of his apartment on New Year's Day, 1997.

Remember Sammy SexMachine? That would be me for the next several months. The anger that I felt from investing almost a decade of my life in a relationship that ended channeled itself into sexual aggression . . . and an onslaught of partners. It wasn't a period of my life when I was particularly patient, responsible, or respectful, although I certainly didn't have a problem extending myself! I won't bore or perhaps titillate you with the details. I also felt a deep sadness over the loss of that relationship. Let's just say that it was very challenging for me to live in the now at that time. Then I pulled myself together, and . . .

The year 2000. The new millennium. Enter Dennis into my life. What can I say? (I'd better say something good . . . he's looking over my shoulder right now! . . . OK, good! Now he's gone . . .) There are so many reasons I feel blessed to be with Dennis. OK, here are just a few. He has a beautiful soul and a true love of life. I like the person I am with him and how I feel. He has an infectious smile that lights up a room. We're free to be ourselves and to open up emotionally to each other. He wants me to be the best I can be, and I want the same for him. I've learned a lot about what it really means to commit, and I'm grateful. I truly enjoy our life together. We recently celebrated our seven-year anniversary. Thanks, Dennis, for sharing your life with me.

CONCLUSION

Just some final thoughts to take with you . . .

Every date is a fresh, new experience, different from the last.

Be real and take it one step at a time.

There may be a connection with him that is unexpected—be open to that.

You can't control the situation or outcome, so relax, enjoy, and let it unfold as it will.

Remember the amazing and compassionate man that you are.

Treat yourself well—and treat him well too.

Thanks for taking this journey with me. I really am very fortunate. How often does a guy get the chance to chronicle the essence of his life's work?

I wish you continued success, fulfillment, and joy. Congratulations from the Gay Matchmaker!

ACKNOWLEDGMENTS

Thank you, to:

Joseph Pittman at Alyson Books, who fortuitously approached me and made this book possible;

Mitchell Waters, our wonderful agent at Curtis Brown, who believed in it from the start;

John W., who was there in 1985 to create ManMate with me . . . and make me laugh a lot;

Graf Mouen, technical specialist, programming wizard and faithful friend, who has been there from day one; and his partner and my friend, Steven Glick, who completes a beautiful pair and was one of my early success stories;

Kevin McAnarney of KPA Associates, for his phenomenal help with public relations and continued support;

Jed Mattes, Fred Morris, Eric Marcus, and Steve Korte, who encouraged me at the beginning;

Scott Enos and Virgil Wong, ingenious webmasters;

Dave Volkman, who started one incarnation of this book with me and now makes a phenomenal financial advisor;

Will Swift, gifted psychologist and friend, who presented years of fun-filled dating workshops with me;

Greg Miller, fabulous graphic designer and host, who approached me to collaborate on ManMate Dinners for 8;

The Lesbian, Gay, Bisexual, and Transgender Community Center of New York, for wonderfully accommodating my numerous dating workshops through the years;

Paul Tenaglia and Unity Church of New York, for inspiration and the opportunity to spread the word in workshops and classes;

Marjorie Roop, who's been a guiding presence for me through the past decade, and whom I entrusted with the first reading of this book;

Bradley Jones, who's extraordinarily been there for me for the past several years;

My family: my dad George, my mom Macy, my aunt Margy, my sisters Marg and Pam, brother-in-law Martin, my nieces Amalia and Lucia, and my friend since childhood, Jane Stageberg, for all their love and support;

My great buddies, Lee Chew, Eric Williams, and Steve Hauck;

Catherine (Cat) Reynolds McLeod, my first (and last!) actual girlfriend, and still an inspiring kindred spirit;

Von Rae Wood, my oldest girl friend in NYC, who's been a ray of sunshine in my life, and who originally came up with the name "ManMate" . . . in about 5 seconds;

My invaluable and incredibly fun assistants of the last twenty-plus years: currently, Michael Vaccaro; most recently and going backward, Denton T., Steve B., Kristopher McD., Jonathan Van D., Bob H., Danny W., Eric Z., AJ M., Frank L., Seth S., Kent M., Seth A., Michael B., Gary K., Jim R., Justin B., Anthony T., Harte K., Terry F., David McD., Todd G., Bill R., Ed W., Ed Z., Paul S., Raphael H., Blake W., Dave E., Alec B., Bill C., Brooks B., David M., Michael H., Brett L., Don S., Doug T., David W., David P., Bill F., Manny F., Ric R., and Lee C.;

The more than five thousand ManMate clients for their illuminating stories, inspiration, trust, and support; and

Dennis Courtney, my cherished partner. This book would not have happened without you. My eternal thanks and love.

ABOUT THE AUTHORS

Grant Wheaton is the owner and founder of ManMate, the oldest and largest personalized gay introduction service in America. Since 1985, he has met and worked with over five thousand men and successfully introduced many hundreds of couples and soul mates in the process. Grant has been dubbed "the Dolly Levi for Gay New Yorkers" by the press. For over fifteen years, he has continued to conduct highly popular dating and relationship workshops and classes. Grant has written advice columns and consults with and coaches clients on a regular basis. His enthusiasm and expertise as a dating and relationship specialist have prompted a recent magazine reporter to exclaim, "Thank God for Grant Wheaton!" He has also worked extensively as an actor—onstage and in numerous films, daytime soaps, and commercials. Grant lives in New York City.

For further information on Grant Wheaton or Man-Mate, Inc.,

call 212-564-4025,

send an e-mail to Grantwwheaton@aol.com,

or visit our website at www.manmate.com.

PHOTO BY MATT LINDSEY

As a writer, Dennis Courtney contributes treatments and special material for many entertainment events in both corporate and theatrical venues. He also works as a "script doctor" and has been critically acclaimed for writing original revues that have been produced across the United States. Dennis is also a nationally known award winning stage director, choreographer, and figure skater. As a performer, he has appeared in numerous Broadway and national touring shows. Dennis is based in New York City.

Representation: Ron Gwiazda, Abrams Artists
Phone: 646-461-9325
E-mail: Denncourt@aol.com
Website: www.denniscourtney.com